I0757041

Development and Policy Dialogue: Contemporary Insights

Thomas Kaydor, Jr.

authorHOUSE®

AuthorHouse™
1663 Liberty Drive
Bloomington, IN 47403
www.authorhouse.com
Phone: 1 (800) 839-8640

Published by AuthorHouse 06/04/2020

ISBN: 978-1-7283-6308-0 (sc)
ISBN: 978-1-7283-6333-2 (e)

Print information available on the last page.

DEDICATION

I dedicate this book to the Governments and peoples of Australia and Liberia; the victims of poverty; and to all those working to alleviate extreme poverty, hunger and disease globally.

CONTENTS

INTRODUCTION

We live in a time when the largest numbers of people are being lifted out of absolute poverty in a relatively short time span in human history. This is happening in Asia and in Africa. This is a time when the understanding of development and the topics for development studies are enriched at an unprecedented pace. This is also a time when the dynamic and thriving economic and social changes in developing countries become inspiration for each other or even for the developed world. The experience and efforts of the developing countries to achieve prosperity, social inclusiveness and good governance have gained greater attention than ever. The diverse paths and innovative approaches taken in many of these countries become important cases of study.

To a great extent, the economic recessions and the social problems in the developed world have left more room for, or even pushed developing countries to reflect on the paths to take in the future in terms of development. These can be about: the relationship between economic growth and social development, the relationship between the state and business (, big businesses), the structure of governance, and the approaches to policy learning. These are in no ways suggesting alternatives to the core values for development. The goals, solutions to the problems, and the sources of these solutions can be a lot more varied.

Tom Kaydor was my student at Crawford School of Public Policy at Australian National University. I was his professor of the courses on development policy and on urbanisation. On the first day when the development course started on a summer morning of the Southern Hemisphere in 2014, Tom managed to catch my attention in a packed classroom. He was keen to interact with me and other students and was vocal about what he thought was right and wrong about the theories on development we had yet started to go through. He was clearly concerned about his country and wanted to express the view or multiple views of people from Africa. His passion also influenced other students in class. I was very happy to engage in the conversation, and at the same time became aware that this was a group of students who were frustrated with the history, excited about the present and deeply anxious about the future of their home. The energy these students have shown reflects the energy of their promising homeland.

Tom told me that he is publishing a book and asked me to write an introduction for it. I am delighted and agreed. The essays in this book reflect on the goals, issues and practices in the fields of development, public administration and international relations with particular interests on Liberia or lessons he thinks Liberia should learn from other countries. It is his take on these topics after studying at Crawford School of Australian National University, where he did not only attend lectures, but also had the opportunity to exchange ideas with his fellow students who are from different parts of the world with rich experience in field of development. The essays convey Tom's enthusiasm in making his voice heard internationally. Now, Tom is working as the Deputy Foreign Minister for International Cooperation and Economic Integration back in his home country (Liberia). His experience will continue to enrich his understanding of these topics. I look forward to the publication of this book and wish him to produce more works in the future.

Professor Bingqin Li (PhD)
Associate Professor, Policy and Governance (POGO)
Crawford School of Economics and Government
Australian National University

PART I

POVERTY ALLEVIATION

HAVE WE FAILED VERY BADLY IN THE FIGHT AGAINST GLOBAL POVERTY IN TERMS OF AID EFFECTIVENESS?

1. INTRODUCTION

The fight against global poverty has come a long way. The Millennium Development Goals (MDGs) were the latest effort to combat global poverty (Annan 2000). As the MDGs expired in 2015, a new global development agenda, the Sustainable Development Goals (SDGs) have been developed (United Nations 2014). Developed countries continue to provide overseas development assistance (ODA) or aid to help developing countries overcome extreme poverty. Aid is 'a sum of concessional loans and grants given to poor countries' (Moyo 2009, p.7). 'Concessional loans are monies lent at below market interests' rates for longer periods than ordinary commercial loans, while grants are monies given for "nothing" in return'. (p. 7). Aid is divided into three components. First, humanitarian aid is provided in response to catastrophes and calamities like the ebola virus disease outbreak in West Africa, flus, earthquakes and tsunamis (Riddle 2014). Second, charity-based aid is disbursed through charitable organizations to the needy (Moyo 2009). Last, 'systematic aid is payments made to recipient countries through bilateral or multilateral channels' (P.7).

Aid is a post-World War II phenomenon which began with the Marshal Plan aimed at Europe's reconstruction (OECD 2014). Following the reconstruction of Europe, the OECD was founded in 1961 to help newly independent and poor countries undertake development programmes (OECD 2014). Presently, these traditional donors have been joined by new ones in providing aid to developing countries. This essay examines whether the world has failed very badly in the fight against global poverty in terms of aid effectiveness. It argues that the world has not failed so baldly in using aid to fight against global poverty, but that donors and recipient countries need to target aid at programmes that directly get the poor out of absolute poverty in low-income countries (LICs), and narrow the inequality gap in middle-income countries (MICs).

2. GLOBAL DEVELOPMENT EFFORTS TO END EXTREME POVERTY

The developed world, the World Bank (WB) and the International Monetary Fund (IMF) have used many strategies to deliver ODA to developing countries. First, the basic needs strategy was adopted in the 1970s-1980s (Haynes 2008). This strategy called for synergies between 'national development policies, local community development needs, and international development assistance' (p. 29). It focused on the provision of sufficient food, clean water, adequate shelter, primary health care, and at least elementary education for the poor (Stewart 2006). This strategy failed because it was subsumed into the Cold War ideological divide which made aid a political tool rather than a developmental one (Thomas 2005), and due to misappropriation of aid by elites in the developing countries (Haynes 2008). Second, the Structural Adjustment Programme (SAP) was adopted in the 1980s-90s (Haynes 2008). It 'encouraged fiscal and monetary discipline, free trade, free capital flow and economic cooperation among states' (p.30). Aid was preconditioned on private sector led development, spending cuts on basic services, reduced wages, limited state intervention in markets, and trade liberalization (Haynes 2005). The SAP also failed because 'it was externally imposed on developing countries, and its increased poverty in poor states' (Haynes 2008, p.31).

Third, the 'Washington Consensus replaced the SAP in the 1990s-2000' (Thomas & Reader 2001, p.79). It assumed that growth and development are contingent on "good policies" and "good institutions" (Haynes 2008). Good policies meant 'stable macroeconomic policies, liberal trade and investment, privatization, deregulation of state-owned assets; while good institutions meant democratic governance, secured property rights, independent central banks and transparent cooperate governance' (P.33). The Washington Consensus arguably failed because it ignored the strategic role of the state and non-state actors in delivering human development goals (Haynes 2008), though Williamson (2005) argues that this was not a 'global policy prescription, but rather a measure for Latin American countries that faced economic challenges beginning 1989'(p.33). Notwithstanding, some components of the Washington Consensus like secured property rights, independent central banks, stable macroeconomic policies, et al. remain relevant to date.

The SDGs are the current global poverty reduction strategy. Goal seventeen calls for global partnership for development. Developed countries commit to develop open, rule-based, predictable, non-discriminatory trading and financial system; address special needs of least developed and landlocked countries, and small island states, and deal comprehensively with developing countries' debt. Under the MDGs, 'only four targets were met' (WB 2013, p. 4). Thus, the successes and failures of the MDGs sparked controversy. For instance, Munoz (2008) argued that Africa failed to meet the MDGs because it had poor starting conditions including weak institutions, conflict, and inflexible assistance' (p. 1). This argument sounds good because all regions had different levels of socio-economic and political conditions (Easterly 2009), hence the need to have disaggregated set targets based on the reality in regions and states. However, poor starting conditions cannot be an excuse for Africa and other regions doing poorly in meeting the MDGs. Poor countries need to take responsibility of their own development priorities as agreed in the Accra Agenda for Action (2008). Conversely, Poku and Whitman (2011) argue that the MDGs have significantly reduced global poverty. Those living 'below US$1 daily fell from 40 per cent in 1981 to 18 per cent in 2004, and US$2 daily fell from 67 to 48 per cent in said period' (Chen & Ravaillon 2007, p.1). Without the MDGs, the current levels of global poverty reduction would not have been possible (Vandemoortele 2011, Ratzan, S 2010). However, 'global poverty has reduced mainly due to growth in China and India, but there will still be more than 700m people living less than US$1 a day by 2015' (Chen & Ravaillon 2007, p.1-2).

In 2013, US$134.8b of net ODA was spent on developing countries (OECD 2013). This shows a decline in aid to LICs and fragile states and tends to support claims that developed countries exploit poorer countries whereby more resources leave developing countries to support development in rich states. For example, Health Poverty Action (2014) argues that 'Sub-Saharan Africa receives US$134b each year in aid, but US$192b; hence a negative ODA balance of US$58b' (pp. 5-6). Most OECD countries have defaulted on the 0.7 per cent of GNI committed to help developing countries (UN Millennium Project 2006). Only Denmark, Luxembourg, the Netherlands, Norway, Sweden and UK have met the target. The US, Germany, France, Japan and the rest have defaulted (UN 2013; Santamaria 2014). This raises further questions about the developed countries' commitment to help their poor counterparts. It has also sparked debate about the relevance of aid among scholars like Jeffry Sachs, William Easterly, Paul Collier, Dambisa Moyo, Roger Riddle, et al.

3. ANALYSIS OF THEORETICAL DEBATES ON AID EFFECTIVENESS

Jeffery Sachs (2005) argues that developing countries are caught in poverty trap, physical geographic trap, landlocked country trap, fiscal trap, governance trap, cultural barriers, geopolitical trap, lack of innovation, and demographic trap. He asserts that 'poverty itself can be a trap caused by a lack of capital per person' (p. 56). This means that the poor do not save enough physical and human capital because their entire income is spent on survival. Sachs (2005) concludes that 'before the poor can get out of the poverty trap, they need a "Big Push" financed by increased foreign aid (p. 246). Although Sachs (2005) recommends increased aid to address global poverty, he downplays concerns about recipient countries' ability to effectively manage aid. If ODA will be mismanaged and cannot be used to reduce poverty in poor countries, then there should be no need for aid.

William Easterly (2006) dismisses the concept of poverty trap arguing that over the last 50 years, GDP per capita in sub-Sahara Africa has increased despite high fluctuations in growth rates. He maintains that poverty traps are not an outcome of zero growth in low income countries, and that 'poor countries have experienced growth between 1950 and 1970 at 1.9 per cent annually but have failed to utilize said growth for poverty alleviation' (P.11). Therefor it is not the lack of resources that keeps poor countries poor; weak institutions and corruption do. The 'stagnation of the poorest countries has more to do with awful government than with a poverty trap' (pp. 42-43). For instance, countries with high corruption levels grow 1.3 per cent less than those with low corruption levels (Easterly 2006). The lack of effective socio-political and economic institutions leads to high levels of corruption and state failures in poor countries. Poor states must therefore build effective institutions to achieve growth and reduce extreme poverty. Effective institutions will allow the 'poor people take initiatives without experts telling them what to do' (Easterly 2009, pp. 77-79). However, home grown initiatives and the innovative ideas of the poor often perish due to the lack of physical capital to start up. Therefore, the poor need more aid to start up and get out of poverty (Sachs 2005).

For his part, Paul Collier (2007) argues that over 980m people are 'trapped in poverty and are heading towards a black hole' (pp.6-7). Africa hosts '70 per cent of these poor; hence the continent is the core of the problem' (p.7). The 'bottom billion are caught in either one of four poverty traps including conflict, lack of natural resources, bad governance and landlocked geography' (p.5). These countries 'have had no growth, and poverty cannot become a history unless the bottom billion grow' (pp.11-12). The world needs to focus on them by helping poor countries develop policies that give the poor and their children voice, hope and the opportunity to grow and prosper. Such help must be effectively provided by developed countries, and efficiently managed by developing countries.

Dambisa Moyo (2009) Argues that aid 'imposes unbearable debts which become a silent killer in poor states, make governments "dull", and increase corruption amongst elites' (p.56). She contends that governments use aid to 'fund public sector employment, and replace national revenues thereby leading to a 'vicious cycle of aid whereby recipient countries become dependent, as donors enslave poor countries through foreign debt' (pp.

48-50). Moyo (2009) believes that 'aid breeds civil wars, diminishes social capital, undermines the effectiveness of civil society, reduces savings and investments, causes inflation, chokes exports, and provides resources for corruption' (p.52). These arguments sound reasonable but tend to ignore the enormous contributions development aid makes to poor states including fragile ones. For example, '38 per cent of ODA was devoted to fragile states while 31 per cent was earmarked for all other countries' (Fragile States 2014, p.24). Cutting aid from these fragile states would further drive them into misery and extreme human suffering. Therefore, Moyo's (2009) argument should not be the basis for cutting aid to poor countries, rather aid should be increased, effectively delivered and efficiently managed by targeting initiatives that directly lift the poor out of poverty.

4. ODA ACCOMPLISHMENTS AND CHALLENGES

Aid has some positive impacts in developing countries, though its correlation with poverty reduction still demands more empirical research (Riddell 2014). First, ODA avails funding to undertake discrete development projects like building of schools, clinics, hospitals, roads, bridges, and provision of electricity and safe drinking water (Riddell 2014). Second, aid is used to support refugees, displaced persons, fight diseases, and address disasters (Riddell 2014). Third, it sometimes funds national budgets thereby bridging funding gaps for development programmes in poor countries. For example, donors like the US, EU, WB, and IMF provide direct budget support to fund poor countries' health sector (WHO 2008, p.4). Fourth, ODA helps to build capacity of developing countries. For instance, the Australian Award scholarship trains citizens of developing countries to support their development initiatives (Australia Awards 2014). Fifth, ODA supports developing countries to meet international development targets. Sixth, donors support civil society organizations (CSOs) to undertake development projects, and advocate for transparency and accountability (Riddell 2014).

Conversely, Riddle (2014) argues 'that aid works, but neither reaches nor assists the poorest and most marginalized' (P. 7). Moyo (2009) argues that donors continue to give aid amidst its failure because 'donors on ODA to pay the salaries of at least 500,000 staff of WB, IMF, UN agencies and registered NGOs' (p.54). Many times, aid monies are wrongly targeted towards priorities unimportant to recipients and therefore sometimes corrupted (Moyo 2009). This ties in with donors' preconditions for aid, which compels recipient countries to agree with donor priorities instead of national development goals. Also, multilateral management of aid undermines recipients' ability to effectively monitor aid flows and develop national capacity to lead development programmes formulation and implementation (Riddell 2014). This also leads to 'lack of hard data to measure impact of aid on poverty reduction, hindering evidence to determine whether development outcomes are caused by aid or other factors' (p. 8). Sometimes donors' default on funding pledges (Sachs 2005).

These problems associated with ODA increase the need for effective aid management. Donors themselves have acknowledged some of these challenges and have therefore initiated aid effectiveness strategies as agreed in the Rome Declaration (2003), Paris Declaration (2005), the Accra Agenda for Action (2008), the Busan Partnership Agreement (2011) and the New DEAL for fragile states (UNU 2012). Both donors and recipients agree on the use of country systems and program-based approaches, demand driven capacity development, increased aid predictability and transparency of aid flows, donor harmonization to reduce aid fragmentation, and inclusion of private sector and businesses in aid coordination and delivery. The CSOs must hold both donors and recipients accountable. Furthermore, to make aid effective, three fundamental issues need to be addressed.

First, aid must address current global poverty dynamics. In 1990, about 93 per cent of the world's poor lived in LICs and one-third lived in fragile states; but presently three-fourth lives in middle income countries (MICs) while only one-third lives in LICs, and 23 per cent in fragile states (Sumner 2010). These changes challenge the future design of poverty reduction policies and aid delivery. This heterogeneous poverty context demands that ODA is diversified to strategically meet the needs of MICs and LICs. The problems of MICs are not necessarily the lack of resources, but rather the equitable distribution of resources and the inability of governments to undertake pro-poor and inclusive growth, build effective institutions, and capacitate the poor. Therefore, aid to MICs needs to address social exclusion and inequality to ensure that the benefits of growth are equitably shared amongst all citizens. For LDCs, aid needs to focus on social safety nets, social protection, and the determinants of growth including education, health, effective institutions, food security, technology transfer, export promotion and fiscal as well as monetary policy reforms (Growth Commission 2008).

Second, the emergence of non-traditional donors leads to competition in the aid market. Woods (2008) and Kondoh et al. (2010) argue that these new donors provide more aid alternatives for development. However, Naim (2007) argues that they undermine aid effectiveness and promotes bad governance, autocracy, corruption, et al. in developing countries. According to Sato et al. (2010), this competition might crowd out old donors, and make aid less effective due to unconditional aid modalities by new donors. However, these arguments are contestable due to the following reasons. First, no aid is unconditional. For instance, Chinese government aid is said to be unconditional, but it requires recipient countries to sever all ties with Taiwan. Using aid to restrict the sovereign powers of poor countries from recognizing Taiwan is more conditional then making democracy and human rights a prerequisite to aid. Second, while net ODA was US134b in 2013, China's aid to Sub-Sahara Africa alone was US$ USD210.2b in the same year (Xinhua Global Times 2014). Most of China's aid as well as aid from India, Brazil, Russia, and other new donors fund infrastructural projects that traditional donors do not fund. Most developing countries therefore favour the new donors who support such infrastructure projects that national budgets cannot undertake. Third, aid is based on moral, economic and political persuasions; hence no country or group should control the aid environment. The traditional donors must see new ones as partners in development rather than competitors undermining the aid landscape. Both old and new donors need to build synergies and effectively deliver aid to poor countries as agreed under the aid effectiveness modalities.

Last, aid to fragile states needs to mitigate humanitarian crisis and simultaneously address causes of fragility. Fragile states' governments do not have the capacity to deliver core state functions (Fragile States 2014). Many are 'recovering from conflict and embarking on peace and state building processes, experiencing long term or recurrent conflicts, insecurity, or high levels of criminality and violence' (p.16). About 1.5b people live in fragile states, 70 per cent of which have experienced conflicts since 1989.

Presently, 30 per cent of ODA is spent on 51 fragile states (OECD 2014). This amount is infinitesimal for states that lack the capacity to govern and provide basic social services to their people. Today, '37 per cent of the world's extreme poor lives in fragile states; and might increase to 50 per cent by 2018 and 75 per cent by 2030' (p. 19). Additionally, fragile states lack transparent, and accountable systems to distribute resources, and are forced to institute generous tax exemptions for FDI attraction which affects tax base thereby undermining citizens' tax payment. They experience distrust in governments, capital flight, high levels of corruption, criminal activities, money laundry and bribery. Stability and development cannot obtain amidst such challenges. Therefore, donors and fragile states must focus more on peace building and state building goals, country-led and country owned transitions out of fragility, effective resource management, alignment of aid with development priorities addressing root causes of conflict, building of trust with emphasis on legitimate politics, peace and security, justice, and economic transformation (Fragile States 2014).

5. CONCLUSION

Global poverty has reduced mainly due to the growth achievements in China and India (Chen & Ravaillon 2007), but poverty is increasing in Africa and other regions (Collier 2007). Aid positively impacts on extreme poverty, though empirical evidence is required to claim causality (Riddell 2014). However, the 'fundamental question is not whether aid works, but rather how aid can be made more effective' (p.17). Although Moyo (2009) and others condemn systematic aid, their deliberate attempt to ignore the significant impact of humanitarian aid undermines such criticisms because there is no fundamental difference between humanitarian and systematic aid. The former addresses emergencies and fragility, while the latter consolidates development initiatives. Fragile states cannot embark on development without stability, and stability cannot be guaranteed amidst widespread poverty. Instability, fragility and poverty are therefore symbiotic, and must urgently be addressed as a global public good. Developed countries must cancel poor countries' long termed debt that made no quantum impact on national development. They must provide more aid to assist LICs and MICs achieve strategic pro-poor and inclusive growth to alleviate extreme poverty (Sachs 2005, 2008).

Finally, institutions are one of the deep determinants of growth (Rodrik 2003, Easterly 2006, and Acemoglu & Robinson 2012). Therefore, to alleviate poverty, developing countries must build inclusive and effective institutions that will protect property rights, law and order, ensure macroeconomic stability, provide public goods and services, and invest mainly in education, health, food security and basic infrastructure to achieve growth. Effective institutions guarantee freedom for the poor, and freedom helps them achieve their capabilities and functioning (Sen 1999). Donors must therefore support the building of effective and inclusive institutions in developing countries. Donors must diversify aid delivery to LICs, MICs and fragile states on a need basis. Traditional and new donors must build synergies to effectively deliver aid, while developing countries' governments must target aid towards projects that directly impact the lives of the extreme poor and marginalized. Indeed, the world has not failed so baldly in using aid to fight against global poverty, but donor and recipient countries must target aid at the needs of the extreme poor, vulnerable and excluded to alleviate global poverty.

References

Accra Agenda for Action 2008, viewed 10 October 2014, <effectivecooperation.org/files/resources/Accra%20Agenda%20for%20 Action%20in%20Brief%20ENGLISH.pdf>.

Acemoglu, D, Robinson, J 2012, *Why nations fail: the origins of power, prosperity and poverty*, Crown Publishers, USA.

africasacountry.com 2014, There is no ebola here: what Liberia teaches us about aid;
Africasacountry (online edition), 19 October, viewed 19 October 2014, <africasacountry.com/there-is-no-ebola-here-what-liberia-teaches-us-about-the-failures-of-aid/>.

Annan, K 2000, *We the peoples: the role of the United Nations in the 21st century*, United Nations, New York, viewed 27 October 2014, <www.un.org/en/events/pastevents/pdfs/We_The_Peoples.pdf>.

Antunes, A, Carrin, G, Evans, D 2008, General budget support in developing countries: ensuring the health sector's interest, World Health Organization, Geneva, viewed 1 October 2014, <www.who.int/health_financing/documents/pb_e_08_2-budget_ support.pdf>.

Australian Awards 2014, Government of Australia, viewed 27 October 2-14, <www.australiaawardsafrica.org/about-australia/>.

Busan Partnership Agreement 2011, *Fourth High Level Forum on Aid Effectiveness, OECD*, viewed 1 October 2014, <www.oecd.org/dac/effectiveness/fourthhighlevelforumonaideffectiveness. htm>.

Chibba, M 2011, 'The Millennium Development Goals: key current issues and challenges', *Development Policy Review*, vol.29, no.1, pp. 75-90.

Collier, P 2007, The bottom billion: why the poorest countries are failing and what can be done about it, Oxford University Press, USA.

Commission on Growth and Development 2008, *The policy ingredients of growth strategies, Part 2, The Growth Report: Strategies for sustained growth and inclusive development*, pp. 33-69, The World Bank.

Easterly, W 2005, 'Reliving the '50s: The big push, poverty traps, and takeoffs in economic development'. Working Papers no. 65, Center for Global Development.

Easterly, W 2006, *The White Man's Burden: why the west's efforts to aid the rest have done so much ill and so little good*, New York: Penguin Books.

Easterly, W 2009, 'The poor man's burden', Foreign Policy, Issue 170, pp.77-81.

Haynes, J 2008, *Development studies: short introductions*, Polity Press, Cambridge.

Haynes, J 2005, *Comparative politics in a globalizing world*, Polity Press, Cambridge.
Health Poverty Action (2014), *Honest Accounts? The true story of Africa's billion dollars loses*; London, UK, viewed 10 October 2014, <www.healthpovertyaction.org/wp-content/uploads/downloads/2014/07/ Honest-Accounts-report-v4-web.pdf>.

Kondoh, H, Kobayashi, T, Shiga, H, Sato, J (2010). 'Diversity and Transformation
of Aid Patterns in Asia's "Emerging Donors', Japan International Cooperation Agency Research Institute Research Institute, JICA-IR working paper no. 21, October.

Moyo, Dambisa 2009, *Dead aid: why aid is not working and how there is a better way for Africa*, New York, USA.

Munoz, E 2008, 'The Millennium Development Goals: facing down challenges', Briefing Paper, no. 2, Bread for the World Institute, Washington DC.

OECD 2013; *Aid to developing countries rebounds in 2013 to reach an all-time high*, Organization of Economic Cooperation for Development, viewed 20 October 2014, <www.oecd.org/newsroom/aid-to-developing-countries-rebounds-in-2013-to-reach-an-all-time-high.htm>.

______2014, *Fragile states 2014: domestic revenue mobilization in fragile states, Executive Summary, Introduction, Questions 1-3*, POGO 8004 Brick, pp. 362-385.

______2014, *Organization for European Economic Co-operation*, OECD, viewed 15 October 2014, <www.oecd.org/general/organisationforeuropeaneconomicco-operation.htm>.

Poku, Nana & Whitman, Jim 2011, 'The Millennium Development Goals: challenges, prospects & opportunities', *Third World Quarterly*, vol.32, no.1, pp 3-8.

Ratzan, S 2010, 'Testimony on achieving Millennium Development Goals', *Journal of Health Communication*, vol. 15, no. 8, pp. 821-4.

Riddell, R 2014, 'Does foreign aid really work?', Keynote address to the Australian Aid and International Development Workshop, 13 February, Australian National University, Canberra.

Rome Declaration 2003, Rome declaration on harmonization, viewed 2 October 2014, <www.oecd.org/dac/effectiveness/31451637.pdf>.

Sachs, J 2005, *The End of Poverty: Economic Possibilities for Our Time*, The Penguin Press, NY.

Sachs, J 2008, *Commonwealth: Economics for a crowded planet*, Columbia, USA.

Sato, Jin et al. 2010, 'How do "emerging donors" differ from the 'traditional' donors?
Institutional analysis of foreign aid in Cambodia', JICA Working Paper Series.

Sen, A 1999, *Development as freedom*, Oxford University Press, UK.

Rodrik, D 2003, 'What do we learn from country narratives?' in Robrik, D (ed), In Search of prosperity, Princeton University Press.

Santamaria, C 2014, Foreign aid spending by OECD-DAC donors rose to all-time high in 2013, *Devex* (online edition), 9 April, viewed 15 October 2014,
<https://www.devex.com/news/foreign-aid-spending-by-oecd-dac-donors-rose-to-all-time-high-in-2013-83265>.

Stewart, F 2006, 'Basic needs', in D. Clark (ed), *The Elgar Companion to Development Studies*, Cheltenham, UK.

Sumner, A 2010, 'Global poverty and the new bottom billion: three quarters of the world's poor live in middle-income countries', One pager, no. 120, International Policy Center for Inclusive Growth, UNDP, November.

Thomas, S 2005, *The global resurgence of religion and the transformation of International Relations: the struggle for the soul of the Twenty-First Century*, New York and Basingstoke, Palgrave Macmillan, UK.

Thomas, C, Reader, M 2001, 'Development and inequality', in B. White, R. Little and M. Smith (eds), *Issues in World Politics*, Basingstoke, Palgrave, pp.74-92.

The Paris Declaration on Aid Effectiveness, viewed 10 October 2014,
<www.oecd.org/dac/effectiveness/34428351.pdf>.

Naim, M 2007, 'Rogue aid: what's wrong with the foreign aid programs of China, Venezuela, and Saudi Arabia? They are enormously generous. And they are toxic', *Foreign Policy*, March/April, viewed 27 October 2014, <www.foreignpolicy.com/articles/2007/02/14/rogue_aid>.

United Nations 2014, *High Level Panel on Post 2015 Development Agenda*, United Nations, viewed 22 October 2014, <http://www.post2015hlp.org/>.

United Nations 2013, *Millennium Development Goal 8: the global partnership for development: the challenge we face. MDG gap task force report 2013*, United Nations, viewed 15 October 2014, <http://www.un.org/en/development/desa/policy/mdg_gap/mdg_gap2013/mdg_report_2013_en.pdf>.

United Nations 2013, *Millennium Development Goals report*, The United Nations, viewed 27 October 2014, <http://www.un.org/millenniumgoals/pdf/report/report-2013/mdg-report-2013-english.pdf>.

United Nations 2006, *UN Millennium Project 2006*, United Nations, New York, viewed 27 October 2-14, <www.unmillenniumproject.org/press/07.htm>.

United Nations University 2012, What is the new deal with fragile states? Policy Brief, no.1, viewed 20 October 2014, <file:///C:/Users/Helen.garbo/Downloads/UNUpb2012-1.pdf>.

Vandemoortele, J 2011, 'If not the Millennium Development Goals, then what?' *Third World Quarterly*, vol.32, no.1, pp. 9-25.

Williamson, J 2005, 'The Washington Consensus as policy prescription for development', Chapter 3 in Besley, T, and Zagha, R., Development Challenges in the 1990s: leading policymakers speak from experience, World Bank and Oxford University Press.

Woods, N 2008, 'Whose aid? Whose influence? China, emerging donors and the silent revolution in development assistance', *International Affairs*. vol.84, no. 6, pp.1205-1221.

Xinhua Global Times 2013, *China-Africa economic and trade cooperation*, Information office of the State Council, People's Republic of China, viewed 26 October 2014, <www.safpi.org/sites/default/files/publications/China-AfricaEconomicandTradeCooperation.pdf>.

OFFERING CASH TO THE POOR IS NOT ENOUGH. THIS NEEDS TO BE COMPLEMENTED WITH SOCIAL SERVICES TO REALLY HELP THE POOR GET OUT OF POVERTY.

Cash transfer (CT) is a form of social assistance that occurs in three forms. It can be cash given to individual households, cash grants or cash for work and voucher programmes, and cash as an alternative to in-kind transfers such as agricultural inputs or non-food-items (Farrington et al. 2006). These three forms of CT are intended to address risk and reduce chronic poverty and vulnerability. Cash transfers have proven to be a cost-effective intervention for poverty alleviation. Although they have a positive impact on poverty reduction, mainly education and health outcomes, evidence remains inconclusive on the sustainability of such approach especially on sustainable economic growth and development (Arnold et al. 2011). This paper argues that offering cash to the poor is not enough to reduce and alleviate poverty. It proposes that CT should be matched with basic social services like free and compulsory public education, free public health system, and low-cost housing for the poor. Structurally, the paper analyses and synthesises the advantages and drawbacks of CT and recommends free public education and health as well as low cost housing for the poor as a supplementary basic social service package that should be matched with cash transfers if poverty must be contained and alleviated.

Cash transfer (CT) programmes provide basic social protection by giving a set minimum cash amount to vulnerable groups facing significant risks of remaining in or falling into the poverty trap. Such programmes increase poor households' real income as a response to chronic poverty and food insecurity or other development challenges. Cash assistance takes variant forms, such as periodic or occasional needs-based transfers, non-contributory pensions and family allowances in the form of regular or occasional benefits paid to families with children under a certain age, amongst others. This practice has become widespread mainly in developing countries where social cash transfers are linked with certain behavioural requirements. In this regard, cash transfers can be used to increase school enrolment of children from poor families or encourage poor families to do regular medical check-ups. Such cash transfers are called conditional cash transfers (CCT). Mexico was the first country to introduce a nation-wide CCT program in 1997, where cash transfers are conditioned on school attendance by the children of beneficiary households, and regular visits to health centres by household members (Lomeli 2008).

Mexico and Brazil are credited for good implementation in terms of targeting, administration and impact evaluation, raising optimism about a stronger role such programmes can play in poverty alleviation. Cash transfer programmes have a positive impact on poverty alleviation, especially with regards to health and education, and can potentially be used as a rapid and cost-effective tool for poverty reduction. On health-related gains, for instance, a 2008 study estimated that the birth weight of Mexico's CCT programme beneficiaries were on average 127.3 grams higher than non-beneficiaries, and incidence of low birth weight 44.5 per cent lower among beneficiaries. This improvement in birth outcomes was explained by better quality of prenatal care as well as the empowerment of women to demand and negotiate better care from health providers (Barber & Gertler 2008). Additionally, the Mexican CCT programme confirms a significant increase in enrolment rates of girls and boys in primary and secondary schools, with the transition rate to secondary schools for girls increasing by 15 per cent. Nevertheless, it was discovered that the impact of the programme is more limited on the quality of school performances and achievements (Hyun 2008).

Another positive aspect of CT is the impact of non-contributory pension programmes on poverty households. These pension programmes have reduced poverty amongst older people by 19 per cent in South Africa, and 53 percent in Brazil (Schubert 2005). Such outcomes have a trigger down effect on vulnerable children and orphans who normally care for older people in developing countries. Contrary to in-kind benefits that can undermine local production and trade, cash transfers also have a positive spill over on local economy, through a stronger demand for local goods and services and increased investment on the supply side. A Zambian Kalomo pilot case study on social cash transfer reveals that while the local economy was inspired by the buying of essential goods like soap, blankets, food and agricultural inputs, some of the beneficiaries saved cash and later invested in animal husbandry and income generating activities (Schubert 2005). Comparatively, cash transfer intervention is considered cost effective compared to commodity-based assistance programmes whose transaction costs are higher.

For recipients, cash transfers present a more practical and cost-effective solution, as cash is easily carried compared to food that must be transported from the distribution site thus placing additional burden on them. Beneficiaries sometimes trade the commodities at cheaper prices in return for cash to meet their priority needs. This provides beneficiaries with economic freedom, whereby they can decide to ration the utilization of their cash based on equally competing households' needs and preferences.

Despite these recorded gains of social cash transfer programmes, there are a number of drawbacks and challenges limiting CT impact on poverty alleviation. First, it has pitfalls and errors in resource allocation to individuals outside of the targeted population and sometimes excludes legitimate households (Lomeli 2008). These targeting errors normally occur due to wrong programme design and implementation, corruption, fraud, and deficient targeting methodologies. Beneficiary lists are sometimes manipulated through false reporting, bribery, deliberate exclusion of eligible or inclusion of non-eligible households (Van Stolk & Tesliuc 2010). For example, while in the Mexican CCT scheme some of the poorest households and qualified communities were denied health and education services, the Brazilian experience unveils concocted and deliberate targeting errors (UNDP 2006, The World Bank 2007). Second, cash transfers sometimes create inflationary risks that undermine the intended benefits of the program. The injection of cash into the local economy at times causes inflation thereby diminishing beneficiaries' purchasing power, although cash transfers programmes in 15 Southern and Eastern African states show less proof of the causal link between cash transfers and inflation in targeted communities (Devereux et al. 2005).

Third, cash transfer programs are expensive to administer during the start-up, implementation and monitoring stages. However, administrative costs quickly decrease in subsequent years of implementation and reduce the average annual costs over the entire period of implementation. For example, in Mexico, the cost of targeting during the first year of implementation represented 65 per cent of total cost of the programme, followed by monitoring at 8 per cent and actual delivery of transfers at 8 per cent. Three years later, the major cost component of the programme was the actual transfers (41 per cent) followed by monitoring of conditionality (24 per cent), while targeting costs dropped to 11per cent of the program's costs. The cost effectiveness of such approach also depends on the selected payment modality (Hyun 2008; Hevia de la Jarra 2008).

Lastly, CT programmes are associated with security risks and corruption (Grimes et al. 2009). For instance, in Liberia, during the disarmament and demobilization process, a vehicle carrying cash intended for ex-combatants that were rehabilitating highways was ambushed and high jacked by unknown gun men (NCDDRR 2004). In Ethiopia, there was a swap from food to cash transfers in all Red Cross programmes, in order to significantly reduce the theft, fraud and wastage that were associated with food distribution (Harvey 2005). To remedy this situation, CT programmes in post-conflict and emergency contexts use cash vouchers, since well-developed banking systems are usually scarce in such settings (Harvey 2007). Nevertheless, cash transfers have been successful in Indonesia, Thailand, Sri Lanka and India in response to the Tsunami disasters (Gore et al. 2006), and in conflict-affected contexts such as Liberia, Somalia and Afghanistan, though with extreme risk. In these contexts, private remittance companies were used to ensure reliable and safe cash delivery.

Using this analysis on CT, and drawing insights from its merits and demerits, poorer households benefiting from CT programmes experience a significant leap in reducing poverty (Kunnemann et al. 2008). However, cash transfers cannot singularly alleviate poverty because recipient families usually divert the cash received to other pressing problems instead of the purposes for which the cash is intended (Ahmed 2006). Social cash transfers therefore have to be supplemented and matched with the provision of basic social services like free and compulsory public education, free public health and low-cost housing for the poor. With these essential social services, efforts to lift poor households out of poverty through cash transfers will be sustained and poverty will be alleviated in the long run.

Education grants to poor households and school feeding programmes make a significant impact on school enrolment in poorer communities (Arnold et al. 2011), but such programmes are not sustainable because they are cost intensive and short run due to scarce resources. Such interventions therefore occur in emergencies and conflict or post-conflict settings and are cut off once conditions stabilize. These schemes are therefore not the most appropriate right based approach to address illiteracy amongst the poor (Kunnemann et al. 2008). Governments in developing countries should therefore provide free and compulsory public education for vulnerable children whose parents cannot afford the high cost associated with education. With compulsory and free education public school system, governments could ensure that most, if not all, poor parents sent their children to school on a compulsory basis since there would be no fees and tuition payment as prerequisite for enrolment. The enforcement of such policies should entail punishments and sanctions on poor parents who refuse to send their children to school. Sanctions and penalties will incentivise poor parents' decision to implement the government's free and compulsory education policy. Matching cash transfer with free and compulsory public education would thereby guarantee that the cash given poor households is mostly used on feeding, essential goods and income generating initiatives from which the families can gradually get out of entrenched poverty.

Although free and compulsory public education complimented with cash transfers might boost school attendance amongst children of poorer households thereby decreasing illiteracy and ultimately increase living standards of poor families as education empowers the weak, vulnerable and poor health could constitute one of those services on which cash given to poorer families is spent since they normally do not live under healthy conditions and can contract various infectious diseases, like malaria in the case of Africa's poor (Adato et al. 2008). In view of this, free public health programmes should form an additional part of the social service programme package in poor communities (Arnold et al. 2011). If poor households have access to free public health care system, cash given them through the CT schemes would be used either on food or other domestic needs. With free public health and education programmes, households would be better off saving their cash and investing in other income-oriented ventures that will lead to sustained income growth, raise living standard and ultimately reduce and alleviate poverty.

In addition to lack of affordable access to education and health amongst poor households, the lack of affordable housing is usually one of the major problems poorer families face. Poorer households hardly have the means to construct decent homes to live in. Most of them in urban areas live in slum communities amidst poor sanitary conditions and thus risk contraction of infectious diseases leading to premature deaths. Lack of or poor and inadequate housing for poverty households is execrated by lack of money to pay for education and health related costs (Kunnemann et al. 2008). Poor and destitute families consequently live unhealthily in squalors, bear their children who grow up in poor environment and in turn are themselves entrapped in poverty. These children grow up without gaining affordable or no access to education, thus perpetuating the vicious circle of illiteracy amongst the poor. They are entrapped in a poverty web such that public policymakers have initiated the transfer of cash to support the poor meet basic livelihood supplies insufficient for alleviating poverty. These social cash transfer programmes therefore need to be accompanied by a comprehensive social service scheme to include construction of low-cost housing in addition to free public health and education systems for poorer households (Arnold et al. 2011). With decent low-cost housing facilities, free public health care service, and free and compulsory education system, destitute and very poor families will become better off using their cash on food and possibly investment in income generation activities that will create sustained growth, increase wealth and raise living standards amongst the poor.

To conclude, cash transfers to poorer households substantively reduce poverty and pave the way to poverty alleviation (Arnold et al. 2011). However, such programmes are inadequate to alleviate poverty because cash transferred to beneficiaries is used for various competing alternatives and imperatives. Cash transfers alone therefore cannot sustainably reduce, curb or alleviate poverty. In lieu of this, developing countries should design and provide an additional assistance through the provision of free education and health care system, and low-cost housing to compliment CT. A combination of social cash transfers and this basic social service package (free public education and health system, and low-cost housing) will permit poorer households make trade-offs and direct their cash to productive ventures like agricultural activities for food sufficiency and purchase of essential goods to lift them out of poverty. Offering cash to the poor is therefore not enough. This needs to be complemented with basic social services to get the poor out of poverty.

REFERENCES

Adato, M & Hoddinott, J 2008, *Lessons from cash transfers in Africa and elsewhere: impacts on vulnerability, human capital development and food insecurity*, IFPRI Presentation to Regional Inter-governmental Experts Meeting, Cairo, Egypt.

Arnold, C, Conway, T & Greenslade, M 2011, 'Cash transfers literature review', Department of International Development (DFID), University of Sussex, Britain.

Barber, L & Gertler J 2008, *Empowering women: how Mexico's conditional cash transfer program raised parental care quality and birth weight*, viewed 6 April 2014, <http://cega.berkeley.edu/publications/mexicocashtransfer.PDF>.

Devereux, S, Marshall, J, Macskill, J & Pelham, L 2005, *Making cash count: lessons from cash transfers in east and southern Africa for supporting the most vulnerable children and households*, Save the Children UK.

Farrington, J & Slater R 2006, 'Introduction to cash transfers: panacea for poverty reduction or money down the drain?', *Development Policy Review*, vol. 24, no.5, pp. 499-511.

Gore, R & Patel, M 2006, *Cash transfers in emergencies: a review drawing upon the Tsunami and other experience*, UNICEF, Bangkok, Thailand, <http://www.unicef.org/socialpolicy/files/Cash_transfers_in_emergencies_-_A_review_drawing_upon_the_tsunami_and_other_experience.pdf>.

Grimes, M & Wängnerud, L 2009, *Curbing corruption through social welfare program? The effect of Mexico's conditional cash transfer program on good government*, QoG Working Paper Series, viewed 6 April 2014, <http://www.qog.pol.gu.se/working_papers/2009_8_Grimes_Wangnerud.pdf>.

Farrington, J, Harvey, P & Slater, R 2005, *Cash transfers: mere "Gadaffi syndrome" or serious potential for rural rehabilitation and development?*, ODI, viewed 5 April 2014, <http://www.odi.org.uk/resources/download/1039.pdf>.

Harvey, P 2007, *Cash based response in emergencies*, Humanitarian Policy Group, Briefing paper, viewed 5 April 2014, <http://www.odi.org.uk/resources/download/256.pdf>.

Hevia de la Jarra, F 2008, 'Between individual and collective action: citizen participation and public oversight in Mexico's Oportunidades programme, State Reform and Accountability: Brazil, India and Mexico', *International Development Studies*, vol. 38, viewed 20 March 2-14, http://www.scribd.com/doc/10076161/Hevia-Felipe-participation-and-social-accountability-in-progresaoportunidades-mexico.

Hyun, S 2008, *Conditional cash transfers programs: an effective tool for poverty alleviation*, Asian Development Bank Economic and research Department Policy Brief Series N°51, viewed 6 April 2014, <http://www.adb.org/Documents/EDRC/Policy_Briefs/PB051.pdf>.

Kunnemann, R & Leonhard, R 2008, *A human rights view of social cash transfers for achieving the Millennium Development Goals*, Brot Fur die Welt, Stultgart, Germany.

Lomeli, E 2008, 'Conditional cash transfers as social policy in Latin America: an assessment of their contributions and limitations', *Annual Review of Sociology*, vol. 34.

National Commission for Disarmament, Demobilization, Rehabilitation and Reintegration (NCDDRR) 2004, *Annual Report*, NCDDRR. Government of Liberia, Monrovia.

UNDP 2006, *Social protection: the role of cash transfers, poverty in focus: conditional cash transfers in Latin America*, International Poverty Centre, viewed 6 April 2014, <http://www.undp-povertycentre.org/pub/IPCPovertyInFocus8.pdf>.

Schubert, B 2005, *Social cash transfers, reaching the poorest*, GTZ, Germany.

The World Bank 2007, Control and accountability mechanisms CCT: a review of programs in Latin America and the Caribbean's: 7 case studies', *Operational Innovations in Latin America and The Caribbean*, vol. 1, no.1, viewed 1 April 2-14, <http://siteresources.worldbank.org/INTLACREGTOPLABSOCPRO/Resources/CCTReview_FINAL.pdf>.

Van Stolk, C & Tesliuc, D 2010, *Toolkit on tackling error, fraud and corruption in social protection programmes*, World Bank, viewed 19 March 2014, <http://siteresources.worldbank.org/SOCIALPROTECTION/Resources/SP-Discussion-papers/Safety-Nets-DP/1002.pdf>.

Thomas Kaydor, Jr.

THE IMPACT OF POOR INFRASTRUCTURE ON POVERTY REDUCTION IN POST CONFLICT COUNTRIES: THE CASE OF LIBERIA

I. INTRODUCTION

This case study is on the Republic of Liberia, Africa's first independent republic, located on the west coast of Africa. The country maintained an aristocratic republican democracy for 133 unbroken years (Sawyer 1991), but later slipped into a devastating 14 years civil war, which ended in August 2003. The war killed about 250,000 people of the country's four million population, and damaged key infrastructure and basic social services including homes, electricity, education, health and water facilities, bridges, roads, air and seaports, and telecommunication (UN in Liberia 2013). Peace and security have been restored to Liberia, following a transitional government instituted by the Accra Peace Accord, and the holding of free, fair and transparent elections in 2005 (CPA 2003). The first post war elections brought Madam Ellen Johnson Sirleaf, first African female head of state and government, to power (UNSG Report 2006).

Although, with the support of the international community and bilateral partners, the government endeavours to restore Liberia to its pre-war status, efforts to reconstruct the country, create access to basic services, and reduce poverty are challenged by the huge infrastructure deficit caused by the civil war (UN in Liberia 2013). Liberia's current poverty rate is 74.6 per cent in rural areas, 47.7 per cent in urban sectors, and 61.5 per cent average at the national level (LISGIS 2008). The estimated cost of reviving the country's damaged transport, water and energy infrastructure is about 2.5b USD, at a time the country's current national budget is 557m (MOF 2014).

This case study argues that governments strive to reduce poverty is stagnated by poor infrastructure, which creates limited access to basic social services, and impedes economic growth and development. It is assumed that if the country's damaged infrastructure-transport, electricity and water systems-is restored, it will increase access to basic services like water, health and education, spur economic growth and might ultimately reduce poverty. The Problem-Oriented Method (Monash University Library

Nd.) is used to identify and analyse existing infrastructural problems and suggests plausible solutions to resolve them. This case study is limited to the impact of poor transportation, and the lack of electricity and pipe born water on poverty reduction in Liberia. It concludes that the government needs to either use one or a combination of three options: the unbalanced growth and big push concepts or borrow low interest rate loans to address its infrastructural deficit.

II. PROBLEM DEFINITION

Moteff et al. (2004) define infrastructure as 'basic facilities, services, and installations needed for the functioning of a society' (p. 1). Without the basic infrastructure, a given society will not function properly. All developed countries have basic infrastructure in place. Most developing countries that have made significant gains in growth and development have also invested in basic infrastructure as a fulcrum for growth and development. Prior to the civil war, Liberia experienced economic growth. Majority of the population had access to good transport system, electricity, pipe born water, and quality health and education systems. These facilities and services were destroyed by the war. Therefore, Liberia is amongst the 104 states categorized under the Multidimensional Poverty Index (MPI), where about 1.56b people live in multidimensional poverty (HDR 2013). It is part of the states with the highest percentages of MPI, ranking 84 per cent behind Ethiopia with 87 per cent, and leading Mozambique and Sierra Leone with 79 per cent, and 77 per cent respectively (HDI 2013). Despite this alarming poverty picture, the HDI (2013) labels Liberia as one of fourteen countries that have recorded human development gains of more than two per cent annually since 2000. Most of the low HDI states fall in Africa, where many are emerging from long periods of civil conflicts. In spite of this steady progress towards recovery, poverty is widespread and majority of the citizens lack access to basic services in these countries.

III. Poor infrastructure as a challenge to poverty reduction

Poor transport system

Good transport system is the lynchpin in all developed countries. Developing countries need to therefore improve their transport systems to increase access to basic services, and spur economic growth and development, thereby reducing poverty (Moteff et al. 2004). However, Liberia's transport system is poor. Major roads linking rural parts of the country are in a deplorable state. About 51.3 per cent of rural inhabitants are gravely affected by the lack of roads (MPW 2013). According to the Liberia Prioritized Infrastructure Development Programme (2012), about USD 1.2b is required to connect Liberia's 15 counties capitals (p. 14). The poor transport system hinders access to basic services like schools and health. For instance, health indicators show that mortality rate in rural areas is 84 per every 1000 births compared to urban areas where mortality stands at 68 per every 1000 births. Also, maternal mortality is estimated at 994 per 100,000, and under age five mortality is 110 per 1000 births (LDHS 2007; UN One Programme 2013). Most of these maternal and under five mortality rates occur in the rural communities where health facilities and personnel are scarce due to limited access.

Like the health sector, access to quality education is hampered by poor transport system. For example, the Liberia Education Sector Plan (2009) calls for compulsory nine-year basic education, comprising six years of government funded free primary, and three years of junior secondary education completion. Despite this laudable education initiative, majority of rural residents and the urban poor cannot send their children to school due to limited public schools, and the lack of adequately trained teachers in the few existing facilities (UNICEF Liberia 2013). Most Liberian schools are operated by religious institutions or private individuals whose objective is to maximize profit. The current net enrolment in primary school stands at 34 per cent, and grade six completion rate in the entire country is 35 per cent (UN in Liberia 2013). This implies that about 65 per cent of the children in the country are out of school. Amongst these are children who enrol, but dropout due to lack of uniforms, fees, tuition and other basic education materials.

Besides road transport, sea transport is also affected by the war. The Liberian port industry is administered and operated by the National Port Authority (NPA) in keeping with its statutory responsibilities to plan, manage and develop public seaports in Liberia. The Authority manages four ports, namely, the Freeport of Monrovia, the Port of Buchanan, the Port of Greenville, and the Port of Harper (NPA Master Plan 2014). All these ports were destroyed during the civil conflict. The Freeport of Monrovia is the largest and most important of Liberia's four ports. It currently services more than 65 per cent of international trade, followed by the Port of Buchanan, which presently handles 30 per cent of trade (NPA Annual Report 2013). The ports' infrastructure are being rehabilitated, but this requires significant capital investment. A total of USD 99m is required to rehabilitate all four ports (NPA 2013). Limited operation of these sea ports undermines sea transport and international trade.

Poor transport system does not only impeded access to health and education services. It also undermines economic recovery, growth and development in post conflict Liberia by placing constraints on the movement of goods and services (Ministry of Commerce and Industry 2014). The rural residents in the country live mostly on subsistence farming, and some produce cash crops for trade and commerce. Farmers, 75 per cent of the total population, produce goods for consumption and trade their surplus to get necessities unavailable locally (Ministry of Agriculture 2013). Due to the absence of farm to market roads, these rural farmers cannot easily transport goods and services from villages and towns to markets. Most of the goods therefore get spoilt due to the lack of preservation facilities. This hinders increased productivity. The urban poor, for their part, live in slum communities where they are entrapped in hunger, poverty and disease as cheaper food products cannot be found on the local markets. Presently, Liberians living below one USD a day are about 63 per cent, and the population living in extreme poverty stands at 47.9 per cent (LISGIS 2007). Rice, Liberia's staple food, is mainly imported from Asia, and costs USD 50 for 50kg on the local market. Majority of the poor therefore cannot afford to feed themselves and families.

LACK OF SAFE DRINKING WATER

The limited access to safe drinking water is the second problem faced by residents in Liberia (LWSC 2014). Access to piped water fell from 15 per cent of the population in 1986 to less than three per cent in 2008 (LISGIS 2008). Project Liberia (2013) indicates that one in four Liberians has access to safe drinking water. Despite the low record of water and sanitation deliverables under Liberia's reconstruction process, there are some positive outcomes showing improvement. The Ministry of Health and Social Welfare (MOHSW 2011, p. 6-7 citied in IMF 2012 Liberia Country Report) indicates that the share of households with access to clean water increased from 67 to 75 per cent between 2007 and 2009. However, wide disparities exist between urban and rural households. Clean and safe drinking water is mostly obtained from hand pumps and bold holds. Access to sanitary toilet facilities rose from 39 per cent to 50 per cent nationwide, with improvement in rural as well as urban areas (CWIQ 2010, p.120-1 cited in IMF 2012 Country Report). In spite of these improvements, the WHO Country Office in Liberia (2013) reports that half of all Liberians lack access to toilet facilities; hence they either defecate up streams and in open areas. It further informs that outbreaks of water borne diseases, like cholera, occur regularly, and that as many as one in five deaths in Liberia are blamed on water and sanitation problems.

LACK OF ELECTRICITY

The lack of electricity is the third challenge that undermines government's effort to reduce poverty (GOL 2013). Liberia has limited energy output. For example, the pre-war 170-megawatt power generation capacity and national grid were completely destroyed during the civil war; hence a little over 0.1 per cent of households has access to public electricity (LISGIS 2008). This power generation capacity is obtained from diesel generators that produce a little more than two megawatts per million people. It costs USD 0.77 to generate one per kilowatt hour electricity (LEC 2012). This cost is exceptionally high (AICD Diagnostic Report 2010). Power tariff of 0.63 per kilowatt hour is about three times the average for Africa, which is very high by global standards (MLME 2013).

Rehabilitation of the country's singular dam, the Mount Coffee Hydro Plant, is estimated at USD 207m (MOF 2012). However, due to the lack of resources, government has been unable to refurbish the dam since the cessation of the civil conflict. Notwithstanding, the European Central Bank (ECB), Germany and Norway have provided grants of USD 65m, 32m and 75m respectively in 2013. The government has committed USD 45m to compliment the grants, and carry out the reconstruction of the dam, which is expected to be completed by December 2015 (MOF 2014).

The lack of electricity affects the operation of concessionaires and the overall national productive capacity of Liberia. The country has attracted over 16 billion USD in foreign direct investment (Liberia NIC 2014). The FDI is intended to restore Liberia's economy to its pre-war status and set the stage for economic growth and development. The investment attempts to also increase employment directly and indirectly. The anticipated employment will boost households' income and foster other economic opportunities through private sector development. Unfortunately, due to the lack of electricity, majority of the concessionaires have not begun full scale operations to yield the needed resources and employment envisaged in the concession agreements. Concessions that are currently operational in the country face enormous transaction costs due to lack of electricity. Delayed operation retard anticipated employment of some part of the labour force (see annex 1 for expected employment), and the resulting unemployment, mainly amongst the country's growing young population, increases socio-political tensions (UNSRSG Report 2013). These tensions have become a key security concern because demonstrations, riots and political agitation amongst young people could undermine the fragile peace and relapse the country into another round of civil conflict (President Sirleaf State of Nation Address 2014).

IV. THE WAY FORWARD

Even though the challenges discussed above still persist, the government is committed to rebuilding the country, grow its economy and ultimately reduce poverty. It has implemented poverty reduction strategy (PRS) one and two between 2006 and 2012 (IMF Country Report 2013) and aspires to make Liberia a middle-income country by 2030 (Liberia Rising Vision

2030 2013). This vision was set to be achieved in the 1980s, when the country was one of the highest income countries in Africa. In the 1960s, Liberia was on par with Japan's GDP, though the country grew without development (Clower 1966). The country is presently one of 35 low-income countries (LICs) in the world, and one of 26 Sub-Saharan African poor countries (World Bank Report 2010). One key factor challenging this ambitious aspiration of becoming a middle-income country is the huge infrastructure deficit. Hence, the government needs to use either the unbalanced growth concept, the big push philosophy (Hirschman 1958, Kirschna et al. 2005, & Rosenstein-Roden 1943) or low interest loan option to invest in infrastructural development. This might salvage the poor infrastructural challenge, restore basic services, and eventually reduce poverty.

THE UNBALANCED GROWTH CONCEPTS

Due to the lack of resources in the less developed countries, there is need for the government of Liberia to use the unbalanced growth theory, whereby it could create imbalances in the system as the best strategy for growth (Hirschman 1958). This means that the little available funding should be used efficiently in strategic sectors (transport, electricity and water) that might lead to a rippling effect in the economy. Investment should be made in these projects because they have the greatest total number of linkages to induce growth and industrialisation, and lead to poverty reduction (Krishna et al 2005). Although the strategic investment of resources in infrastructure seem the best model, substantive investment in this sector is difficult to achieve due to the lack of financial resources. For instance, Liberia's real GDP is USD 1233; its GDP per capital is USD 328, and the present growth rate is 8.5 per cent (MOF 2014). Despite this impressive growth rate, the country has consecutively experienced budget deficits in three years. Therefore, reliance on this option as the singular approach to addressing the infrastructural deficit might not yield the desired results.

THE BIG PUSH CONCEPT

Giving the lack of adequate national resources to mitigate Liberia's infrastructural deficit, the government should consider the 'big push' option (Rosenstein-Roden's 1957). The idea behind the big push theory is that a country cannot do anything until it can do everything. Outlined by Paul Rosenstein-Rodan (1957), this theory argues that even the simplest activity requires a network of other activities and that individual firms cannot organise such a large network, so the state or some other giant agency must step in. With this background, it might be impossible for the government alone, given its current financial status, to restore the country's damaged infrastructure. Also, private investors will not maximize the desired profits amidst the infrastructure challenge, yet they do not want to risk their capital in public infrastructural. That infrastructure and social services are considered public goods (Gans et al. 2013), private consider investment in such public facilities a government's responsibility. However, as some ground speed is required for the aircraft to airborne, certain critical amount of resources need to be allocated for development activities in Liberia. Therefore, the government, private investor and donors' need to invest in the restoration of transportation, water and energy resources. Concessions could invest some of part of their expected royalties to government in the infrastructural sector. Because no piecemeal allocation in an economy can move on the path of economic development, investment in social overhead capitol is necessary for economic development. With economic growth and development, government can allocate more resources to basic social services, and reduce poverty (Haynes 2008).

LOW INTEREST LOANS

Borrowing of loans is the third option available to the government to mitigate its infrastructural shortfall. Loans could be taken from the World Bank and IMF, and friendly governments to undertake the needed infrastructural projects in the transport, water and electricity sectors. However, the WB and IMF may not be disposed to giving loans to Liberia because they and other partners waived USD 4b debt in 2010 (IMF 2010) and placed a moratorium on the country's borrowing. However, other bilateral partners could lend Liberia interest free loan that might enable the government to develop its national infrastructure, which is very critical to the overall economic growth and the improvement of the people's lives. One of such avenues for interest free or low interest loans is the China-Africa loan facility (FOCAC 2012). In 2006, China's grant assistance, interest free and preferential loans to Africa increased astronomically. In addition, since 2009, China has remained Africa's largest trading partner. In 2013, trade between China and Africa reached USD 210b, unmatched by previous times (Xinhua Global Times 2014). China has expanded cooperation in investment and financing by providing USD 20b of credit line to African countries (FOCAC 2012). Specifically, the China Union has invested USD 2.6b in the Iron Ore mining sector in Liberia (NIC 2012). Liberia supports the 'One China Policy'. The government should therefore take advantage of the cordial bilateral relationship and get Chinese low interest rate loan to fund part of its infrastructural projects.

Additionally, the Liberian government could utilize the Tokyo International Conference on Africa Development (TICAD) process to fund part of its infrastructural projects. The TICAD underscores South-South cooperation and promotes the development of trade and investment between Asia and Africa (TICAD V Report 2013). It recognizes that infrastructure development, including road networks, energy, and access to safe drinking water, is critical to economic integration, trade and investment promotion, and poverty reduction in Africa. Therefore, the Medium to Long Term Strategic Framework (MLTSF) of the TICAD process forms the basis for a coherent strategic approach to the development of infrastructure in Africa. Giving the strong bilateral relationship between Liberia and Japan, the government could also lobby for more funding to complement other funding modalities and address its infrastructural challenges.

V. CONCLUSION

This paper argues that poor infrastructure inhibits economic growth, hinders access to basic social services, and undermines government efforts to reduce poverty in post-conflict Liberia. It points out that prior to the 14 years civil war, Liberia experienced economic growth, and the residents had increased access to basic services. It is therefore plausible that if the country restores good infrastructure (transport, electricity and water systems), it might experience economic growth and development as was in the pre-war status. This might increase accessed to social services and ultimately reduce poverty. To achieve this, the Liberian government needs to either use one or a combination of three options to address its infrastructural deficit. First, it could utilize the unbalanced growth concept by investing its limited resources in the infrastructural sector as a driver to spur economic growth and development. Second, the government could engage in a joint government, private sector and donor partnership to address the infrastructure challenge and restore basic social services through a 'big push' option. Last, it could borrow interest free or low interest rate loans under the China Africa Partnership loan facility, and from the TICAD arrangement to fund some of the country's infrastructural projects. To better coordinate this process and ensure implementation success, the government needs to constitute an inter-ministerial or inter-agency coordinating task force that will adopt the appropriate methodology, and coordinate stake holders in addressing the country's protracted infrastructure dearth.

REFERENCES

Africa Infrastructure Country Diagnostic Report 2010, *Liberia Infrastructure, A continental Perspective*, viewed 7 May 2014, <http://siteresources.worldbank.org/INTAFRICA/Resources/Liberia-Country_Report_03.2011.pdf>.

Accra Comprehensive Peace Agreement on Liberia (CPA) 2003, Accra, Ghana.

Clower R, 1966, *Growth without development: an economic survey of Liberia*, Northwestern University Press, Chicago, USA.

Economic and Social Commission for Asian and the Pacific review report (nd), *Eco-efficient and sustainable urban infrastructure development in Asia and Latin America*, Viewed on 7 March 2014, <http://www.unescap.org/esd/environment/infra/suncheon/background-studies.asp>.

Forum on Chian-Africa cooperation (FOCAC) 2012, 'The fifth ministerial conference of the forum on China-Africa cooperation Beijing action plan (2013–2015)', viewed 8 April 2014,
<http://www.voltairenet.org/article175401.html>.

Gans, J, King, S, Stonecash, R & Mankiw, G 2013, *Principles of Economics*, China Translation and Printing Services, Beijing, China.

Government of Liberia (GOL) 2013, *Executive Mansion website*, Government of Liberia;
< http://www.emansion.gov.lr/>.

Haynes, J 2008, *Development studies: short introductions*, Polity Press, Cambridge, UK.

The International Monetary Fund 2012, *IMF Country Report*, no. 12/45, viewed 30 March 2014;
< www.imf.org/external/pubs/ft/scr/2012/cr1245.pdf>.

Krishna, K, Pérez, C 2005, 'Unbalanced growth', *The Canadian Journal of Economics / Revue canadienne d'Economique,* Vol. 38, No. 3, pp. 832-851.

Ministry of Education 2009, *Liberia Education Sector Plan 2009,* Government of Liberia.

Ministry of Finance, *Agenda for Transformation (AfT) 2013,* Ministry of Finance, Government of Liberia, viewed 7 March 2014,
< mof.gov.lr/doc/AfT%20document-%20April%2015, %202013.pdf>.

Liberia Institute of Statistics and Geo-Information Services (LISGIS) 2007, *Liberia Demographic and Health Survey (2007),* Liberia Institute of Statistics and Geo-Information Services (LISGIS), Monrovia, Liberia.

Liberia Institute of Statistics and Geo-Information Services (LISGIS) 2008, *National Census Report,* Government of Liberia, Monrovia, Liberia. *Liberia Rising Vision 2030* 2013, Ministry of Finance, Government of Liberia, viewed 7 March 2014;
< mof.gov.lr/doc/AfT%20document-%20April%2015, %202013.pdf>.

Government of Liberia 2012, *Liberia Prioritized Infrastructure Development Programme 2012,* Project Development Office, Executive Mansion, Government of Liberia.

Government of Liberia, *National Port Authority (NPA) Master Plan 2014,* Government of Liberia.

Liberia National Investment Commission 2014, Government of Liberia.

Liberia Water and Sewage Cooperation (LWSC) 2014, Government of Liberia.

Ministry of Agriculture (MOA) 2013, Government of Liberia.

Ministry of Commerce and Industry 2014, Government of Liberia.

Ministry of Education 2009, *Education Sector Policy*, Government of Liberia, viewed 31 March 2014, <planipolis.iiep.unesco.org/upload/Liberia/Liberia_Sector_Plan.pdf>.

Ministry of Finance 2014, Government of Liberia.

Ministry of Finance 2012, Government of Liberia.

Ministry of Planning and Economic Affairs 2013, *Republic of Liberia agenda for transformation: steps towards Liberia Rising 2030*, Government of Liberia, viewed 11 March 2014
< mof.gov.lr/doc/AfT%20document-%20April%2015, %202013.pdf>.

Ministry of Public Works 2013, Government of Liberia.

Monash University Library (nd), *How to Write the Case Study, QuickRef27*, viewed 21 March 2014,
<www.monash.edu.au/lls/llonline/quickrefs/27-case-study.pdf>.

Moteff, J and Parfomak, P 2004, *Critical infrastructure and key assets: definition and*
identification, Congressional Research Services, the Library of Congress, viewed 7 March 2014,
< https://www.fas.org/sgp/crs/RL32631.pdf>.

Project Liberia 2014, viewed 21 March 2014,
<http://www.wavesforwater.org/project/Project-Liberia>.

Rosenstein-Rodan 1957, *Notes on the theory of the 'big push"*, Center for International Studies, MIT, USA.

Sawyer, A 1992, *The emergence of autocracy in Liberia: tragedy and challenge*, ICS, San Francisco, California.

The World Bank 2010, *Liberia GPD per capital estimate cited in United Nations in Liberia 2013, One programme: The UN Development Assistance*

Framework (UNDAF 2013-2017), Monrovia, viewed 14 January 2014, <http://unliberia.org/doc/undaf_doc.pdf>.

Tokyo International Conference on Africa Development (TICAD) V Report 2013.

UNDP, *Human Development Report 2013*, UNDP, New York.

UNDP, *Human Development Index 2013*, United Nations Development Programme, New York, viewed 20 March 2014, <http://www.undp.org/content/undp/en/home/presscenter/ pressreleases/2013/03/14/human-development-index-in-2013-report- shows-major-gains-since-2000-in-most-countries-of-south/>.

United Nations in Liberia 2013, One programme: *The UN Development Assistance Framework (UNDAF 2013-2017)*, Monrovia, viewed 14 January 2014, <http://unliberia.org/doc/undaf_doc.pdf>.

United Nations Secretary General Report to the Security Council 2006, New York.

UN Special Representative of the Secretary General (UNSRSG) Report 2013, UN in Liberia.

UNICEF Liberia 2013, Mamba Point, Monrovia, Liberia.

World Health Organization Liberia Country Officer 2013, Mamba Point, Monrovia, Liberia.

World Commission on Environment and Development (WCED) (1987), *Our common Future*, Oxford: Oxford University Press, viewed 10 March 2014, < conspect.nl/pdf/Our_Common_Future-Brundtland_Report_1987.pdf>.

Xinhua Global Times 2014 (April 22) <http://news.xinhuanet.com/english/africa/2014-04/22/c_133281845. htm>.

Thomas Kaydor, Jr.

OBSTACLES TO ACHIEVING SDG TWO IN THE REPUBLIC OF LIBERIA

In 2000, when global leaders agreed on the eight Millennium Development Goals (MDGs), the Republic of Liberia was at war. The fourteen-year civil conflict killed about two hundred-fifty thousand (250,000) persons, and destroyed infrastructures, including schools, roads, ports, hospitals and clinics. Several communities were burnt down thereby uprooting residents and forcing them into exile or displaced camps (Humphreys & Richards 2005). Rebel fighters maimed civilians, kidnapped, raped and impregnated teenage girls. To date, rape remains high in post conflict Liberia, and teenage pregnancy persists thus undermining the advancement of most adolescent girls in the country. Presently, teenage pregnancy rate in the country stands at 31% (United Nations in Liberia 2013).

Following series of negotiations, the African Union (AU), United Nations (UN), and Economic Community for West African States (ECOWAS) brokered a peace agreement in Accra, Ghana in August 2003. This agreement brought an end to the Liberian civil conflict. An Interim Government was set up to disarm, demobilize and reintegrate combatants. It was also given responsibility to conduct free, fair, peaceful and democratic elections in October 2005 (Accra Comprehensive Peace Agreement 2003). After the 2005 general and presidential elections, the country continues to make quantum progress in implementing the MDGs especially goals 3, 4, 6 and 8 (United Nations in Liberia 2013). Despite this impressive progress, Liberia, like many sub-Sahara African states, will not achieve MDG Two on target (Chibba 2011). The two main obstacles to Liberia's achievement of MDG Two are the infrastructural deficit and weak governance capacity inherited from the civil conflict (Munoz 2008). This essay discusses how these obstacles continue to slow the country's progress in achieving universal primary education. It also proffers suggestions on how the state could surmount the obstacles and achieve this goal.

The Liberian civil war destroyed roads, bridges, houses, air and seaports, schools, water pipelines, electricity supply, hospitals and clinics thereby creating a huge infrastructural deficit. The estimated cost of rebuilding

Liberia's damaged infrastructure is about two and half (2.5) billion US Dollars at a time the current national budget of the state is just a little over five hundred million (Ministry of Finance 2013). This infrastructural challenge has an adverse impact on the country's economic development. Currently the country lacks electricity and safe drinking water. Roads linking all the fifteen political subdivisions are in a deplorable state thereby hindering access to schools, clinics, markets and other basic services. Due to lack of electricity, safe drinking water and roads, investment cost remains expensive, and human survival is at risk. The high cost of investment in Liberia leads to stagnated economic growth and development.

Furthermore, the country cannot easily return to its prewar economic growth status. The slow economic growth and development lead to widespread poverty (Collier 2007). Currently, the poverty rate in the country puts those living under one US Dollar a day at 63%, and the population living in extreme poverty remains at 47.9% (Liberia Institute of Statistics and Geo-Information Services 2007). The infrastructural deficit and its accompanying effects, including the lack of enough and quality primary schools in the country, undermine net enrolment and completion of primary education. For example, while primary school net enrolment stands at 34%, the overall grade six completion rate in the entire country lingers at 35% (United Nations in Liberia 2013). Against this backdrop, Liberia will not achieve MDG Two on target.

Although the humongous infrastructural challenge hinders Liberia's drive to achieving MDG Two, weak governance is another key blockage to the country's efforts to achieve universal primary education. The war dealt a deleterious blow on all the socioeconomic and political institutions. It not only destroyed the efficacious functioning of the three branches of government, Executive, Legislature and the Judiciary, but also the conflict rendered key technical national institutions dysfunctional and as well led to high human resource deficit.

For instance, the Ministry of education lacks professional educational administrators and has therefore lost control of its statutory role to effectively coordinate, monitor and foster quality education in the country. The hierarchical structures of the educational system leading from the Ministry to County, district and community education offices remain in the state of recovery. These institutional weaknesses are compounded by low and weak human resource capacities to effectively run schools and efficiently manage classrooms (UNICEF Liberia 2011). Despite government's free and compulsory primary education policy for public schools, majority of primary school age students cannot enroll due to acute shortage of public schools and qualified teachers to manage the limited existing ones. While most of the educational institutions in Liberia are managed by apprentice teachers, the few that deliver quality education are predominantly owned either by religious institutions or private investors whose primary objective is guided by profit motives. Therefore, poor parents cannot not afford to send their children to private institutions. As a result, most of the children in Liberia remain out of school, consequently obstructing Liberia's achievement of universal primary education in 2015.

Even though infrastructural deficit and weak governance impede the achievement of MDG Two in Liberia, the country could reverse the situation and make incremental progress towards achieving MDG Two by taking advantage of two opportunities. First, the international community, which still supports the United Nations Mission in Liberia (UNMIL) as a peace keeping force, takes pride in the nation's recovery. The United Nations considers the restoration of peace and security in Liberia as a success story in the UN's peace keeping history. Hence the presence and concerted engagement of the UN in the country's recovery open a window of opportunity for the government to embark on right-based and results focused development planning through which achievement of MDG Two could be factored in the country's national development agenda as a prime target. Second, that Liberia has benefited debt waiver of over four billion US Dollars (International Monetary Fund 2010), the country has leverage to harness and transparently manage its rich natural resources to spur economic growth and development, which would generate indigenous resources to finance implementation of MDG Two and other development programmes (Turrent & Oketch 2009).

In September 2015, the new global development agenda, the Sustainable Development Goals (SDGs) were agreed. Seventeen goals with 169 targets were set up, and their implementation began on 1 January 2016. Unlike the MDGs under which Goal Two focused on education, Goal Four of the SDGs is focused on quality education. To date, the same constraints and obstacles that prevented Liberia from achieving MDG Two persist.

Worse more, the government has not domesticated the SDGs. Therefore, it would be unlikely for Liberia to achieve universal primary education by 2030. Therefore, it would be good were the government to domesticate the SDGs and progress with the implementation of Goal Four.

Thus far, this essay has discussed infrastructural deficit and weak governance as consequences of the civil conflict obstructing the achievement of MDG Two and posing a challenge to achieving SDG Four in Liberia. It has also highlighted two opportunities that the country could take advantage of to facilitate mitigation of these obstacles. To conclude, the civil war destroyed infrastructure, weakened the political and socioeconomic fabric of the state, and decimated the human resource capacities of the country. However, the country has regained peace and stability and has had a successful democratic transition from one regime to the other over twelve years. Liberia should therefore take three tangible steps in addressing the two main obstacles to achieving MDG Two, and that pose a challenge in achieving SDG Four.

First, to salvage the infrastructural deficit, the country needs to woo donor support and international solidarity to complement national resources that will allow the government to rebuild the damaged infrastructure including primary schools in all communities. Second, the building of more primary schools should simultaneously be carried out with the training of qualified and professional teachers to run those schools. Finally, the country should revamp the Ministry of Education and its local structures to efficaciously coordinate, monitor and administer the provision of quality education for all children in pursuit of attaining universal primary education in the Republic of Liberia.

REFERENCES

Accra Comprehensive Agreement on Liberia 2003, Accra, Ghana, viewed 23 January 2014, <rocesshttp://www.ucdp.uu.se/gpdatabase/peace/Lib%2020030818.pdf>.

Chibba, M 2011, 'The Millennium Development Goals: key current issues and challenges', *Development Policy Review*, vol. 29, no. 1, pp. 75-90.

Collier, P 2007, *The bottom billion: why the poorest countries are failing and what can be done about it*, Oxford University Press, Oxford.

Humphreys. M & Richards, P 2005, 'Prospects and opportunities for achieving the MDGs in post conflict countries: a case study of Sierra Leone and Liberia' Discussion Paper, Columbia University, USA, viewed 17 January 2014 <http://www.columbia.edu/~mh2245/papers1/HR.pdf>.

International Monetary Fund 2010, *'Liberia Wins $4.6 Billion in Debt Relief from IMF, World Bank'*, International Monetary Fund, viewed 1 February 2014, <http://www.imf.org/external/pubs/ft/survey/so/2010/car062910a.htm>.

Liberia Institute of Statistics and Geo-Information Services (LISGIS) 2007, *Liberia Demographic and Health Survey (2007)*, Liberia Institute of Statistics and Geo-Information Services (LISGIS), Monrovia, Liberia.

Ministry of Finance 2013, *'National budget of Liberia'*, Department of Budget, Ministry of Finance, Republic of Liberia, viewed 31 January 2014, <http://www.mof.gov.lr/content.php?sub=120&related=21>.

Munoz, E 2008, 'The Millennium Development Goals: facing down challenges', Briefing Paper no. 2, Bread for the World Institute, Washington DC.

Turrent, V & Oketch, M 2009, 'Financing universal primary education: An analysis of official development assistance in fragile states', *International Journal of Educational Development*, vol. 29, no. 4, pp. 357-365.

UNICEF Liberia 2011, *'Education in emergencies and post-conflict transition: 2010 report evaluation'*, pp. 6-10, viewed 31 January 2014, <http://www.educationandtransition.org/wp-content/uploads/2007/04/Liberia_EEPCT_2010_Report.pdf>.

United Nations in Liberia 2013, *One programme: The UN Development Assistance Framework (UNDAF 2013-2017)*, Monrovia, viewed 14 January 2014, <http://unliberia.org/doc/undaf_doc.pdf>.

PART II

CORRUPTION AND ANTI-CORRUPTION

LIBERIA ANTI-CORRUPTION COMMISSION (LACC) PROSECUTION RATE

1. INTRODUCTION

In 2008, the LACC was established to investigate, prosecute and prevent acts of corruption by educating and informing the public about ills of corruption and the benefits of its eradication (LACC Act 2008). The Commission's mandate is similar to that of the Indonesian Komisi Pemberantasan Korupsi (KPK) modelled on Hong Kong's Independent Commission Against Corruption (ICAC) whose role is focused on 'corruption investigation, prosecution, policy coordination, research and education' (Kuris 2012, p.2). Liberia ACC differs from the New South Wales' Independent Commission against Corruption (ICAC) in that the latter investigates but cannot prosecute.

This research examines why the LACC prosecution rate is low, and discusses the challenges militating against the speedy and successful prosecution of corruption in Liberia. The research is important because the LACC was created to curb the endemic corruption in both the Liberian public and private sectors (LACC Act 2008). Corruption in Liberia, like anywhere else, hampers sustainable socio-political tranquillity and retards economic growth and development of the post-conflict country (UNCAC

2003; LACC Act 2008). In fact, the 12 April military overthrow in 1980 used corruption as a basis for the coup d'état (Liberia Coup D'état 1980; TRC Report 2009), and the 14 years civil conflict which respectively removed Presidents Samuel Kanyon Doe and Charles Taylor also used corruption as a justification for the Liberian civil war from 1989 to 2003 (Cook 2003; TRC Report 2009).

The TI Global Corruption Barometer (2013) rates corruption in Liberia as very corrupt. For example, this corruption barometer rates the Liberian Legislature 96 per cent, police 94 per cent, Judiciary 89 per cent, education 87 per cent, businesses 78 per cent, political parties 71 per cent, public officials and civil servants 67 per cent, media 53 per cent, military 51 per cent, health 49 per cent, NGOs 45 per cent, and religious groups 22 per cent. This essay therefore argues that low prosecution capacity, legal, judicial and political barriers impede the LACC prosecution powers, and thereby undermine the fight against corruption in Liberia. It concludes that persistent widespread corruption in Liberia can only be addressed if the LACC is adequately funded, well-staffed, and gets the political will of political leaders, and when the appropriate legal and judicial frameworks are put in place for its efficacious operation.

2. DEFINITION OF CORRUPTION

To discuss the LACC's prosecution rate, it is important to understand what constitutes corruption in Liberia. The LACC Act considers 'embezzlement, extortion, bribery, fraud, influence peddling, insider trading, misuse of entrusted public property and vested authority, and any economic and financial crimes' as corrupt acts (LACC Act 2008, P. 5). It specifically defines corruption as:

> 'any act or acts, decision or decisions or use of public resource or resources by a public or private official in the discharge of official duties and or responsibilities which, in order to satisfy the selfish desire or interest of the said official or other person or persons, natural or legal, ignore the established laws, regulations, and thereby, deny, deprive, and prevent, the State or person or

persons natural or legal from receiving entitlement, consideration, and or treatment' (P.5).

The Liberian definition of corruption conforms to that of the United Nations Development Program which defines corruption as the 'abuse of public power for private benefit through bribery, extortion, influence peddling, nepotism, fraud, or embezzlement' (UNDP 1999 cited in APEC 2006, p.3). It also entails key elements of Mark Philp's (1997) definitions of political corruption and agrees with TI's definition-the abuse of entrusted power for private gain (TI 2014).

Corruption undermines democracy, sustainable development, rule of law, investment and economic growth, and aggravates poverty (UNCAC 2003; Quah 2003). For example, in India and other countries, the poor have to bribe officials to obtain basic services (P.176). This corrupt behaviour perpetuates poverty as public officials prosper at the detriment of the very poor. Also, the World Bank has estimated that 'the Philippines government "lost" a total of US$48 billion to corruption between 1977 and 1997' thereby undermining the effectiveness and development of the state (World Bank 1997 cited in Quah 2003, p.176). In Liberia, 13 former ministers were executed for 'corruption' after the 12 April military overthrow ((Liberia Coup D'état 1980).

3.   LACC PROSECUTION RATE

Corruption prosecution is a global challenge due to 'the lack of political will which is the lack of commitment of government leaders to eradicate corruption in their countries' (Quah 2003, p. 177), and the difficulty in gathering substantive evidence for prosecution due to cultural norms of individuals not wanting to report their colleagues or relatives (Larmour 2008). Although many countries default on successfully fighting corruption, 'Hong Kong and Singapore have shifted from being corrupt to being relatively clean' (Kaufmann 1997, p. 223). Apparently, it was along the lines of creating a clean government that the LACC was created. However, since its formation in 2008, the Commission has only conducted two prosecutions out of at least 58 cases in 2011 and 2012 (LACC Report 2012). One of these prosecutions initially experienced a hung jury in

2010 but was later won in a lower court. The defendant, 'former Liberia Telecommunications Authority boss, Albert Bropleh has since filed an appeal at the Supreme Court where final judgment is pending' (LACC Report 2012, p.11). The second case against former police chief, 'Munah-Sieh Brown was also won in a lower court, but again, the defendant took an appeal at the high court' (p. 14). Therefore, the LACC has zero success rate of prosecution since its formation because the outcome of the two appeals are still pending at the Supreme Court.

Unlike the very low LACC prosecution rate, the Malaysian Anti-Corruption Commission (MACC) chief, Tan Sri Abu Kassim Mohamed, boasted that his country 'surpassed Hong Kong's fight against graft based on its higher conviction rate, of 85 per cent-five per cent more than the international benchmark for good performance' (Zahiid 2013, p.1). The 'MACC won this 85 per cent prosecution rate out of 701 arrests in 2012', but its critics argue that it only deals with petty corruption, not grand corruption' (p.1). For its part, the Honk Kong Independent Commission Against Corruption investigated and prosecuted 115 cases in 2013, and 158 persons were convicted leading to a person-based conviction rate of 77 per cent, and a cased-based conviction rate of 81 per cent out of a total case load of 1519 (ICAC Fact Sheet 2014). The Hong Kong ICAC is credited for prosecuting both petty and grand corruption. Such successful prosecution and conviction rates are due to adequate anti-corruption measures including sufficient resources, adequate legal and judicial instruments and political will (Quah 2003). These measures are inadequate in Liberia; hence the LACC's binding constraint.

1. LACK OF RESOURCES

The Liberia ACC has a very low resource capacity to prosecute corruption. First, it has very poor human resource capacity. Presently, the Commission has 12 investigators and one lawyer (LACC Report 2012). 'Six of these investigators who were recruited in 2012 are in dying need of training' (pp.31-32). This limited staff capacity cannot allow the Commission to effectively investigate cases of corruption. Twelve investigators cannot handle corruption cases in the nation's capital, needless to talk about the 15 political subdivisions of the country. A single lawyer cannot also prosecute corruption cases for the Commission. It therefore goes without saying that the 'LACC lacks the human resource capacity to investigate and prosecute corruption' (p.31).

The low human resource capacity of the LACC is blamed on inadequate budgetary allocation to the Commission, the second capacity barrier. For instance, following the Commission's 2012 recruitment and employment exercise 'the Ministry of Finance reduced the LACC's budget from US$585,500.00 to only US$350,000.00' (2012 Report, p. 21). This decrease accordingly 'affected the US$150,000.00 placed in core budget for the improvement of the Legal Unit' (p. 21). The Finance Ministry which diverted 'US$235,000.00 of the Commission's approved budget failed to provide information on the whereabouts of this diverted budgetary allocation' (p.21). Therefore, the Commission was 'constrained not only to cancel the creation of 15 county offices, but also it was compelled to employ only seven investigators instead of an original number of ten' during the 2012/2013 fiscal year (p. 21). If an anti-corruption commission's budget could be diverted without explanation by the Ministry of Finance, then it suffices to conclude that the commission is a toothless bulldog, and that there is a sufficient lack of political will to allow it effectively to function.

2.   LEGAL AND JUDICIAL BARRIERS

Besides the capacity deficit negatively impacting the effectiveness of the LACC, there are legal and judicial barriers impeding its work. First, the LACC relies on the Ministry of Justice to prosecute cases. This ministry may decline to prosecute a case of corruption recommended for prosecution if it determines that the evidence adduced by the Commission is manifestly inadequate or illegally acquired (LACC Act 2008). In such case, the 'commission shall be given the opportunity to augment the evidence or to show that the evidence is in fact adequate and properly acquired' (p. 19). Alternatively, upon failure of the Ministry of Justice to prosecute a corruption within three months after the LACC has recommended, the LACC itself can prosecute (pp. 18-20). This was the situation in July 2012. The 'Justice Ministry ignored the LACC objection and dropped charges against the former Inspector General of the Liberian National Police for corruption and irregularities in the procurement of police uniforms' (US

Report 2013, pp.12-13). However, the LACC independently hired private lawyers and prosecuted said case, subsequently obtaining a conviction which has been appealed at the Supreme Court by the defendant. Two years later, the court has not handed down its judgment thereby slowing the fight against corruption.

Apparently frustrated by the noncooperation of the Justice Ministry, the LACC wrote in its 2011 Annual Report as follows:

> 'the date of the submission of each case up this reporting, shows that each case had stayed more than 3 months or 90 days at the Ministry of Justice. According to the LACC Act of 2008, Section 11.4 (a) notwithstanding the above, the Commission may directly prosecute acts of cases of corruption through the courts if the Justice Ministry, for whatever reason (a) does not take action to prosecute a case of corruption forwarded to it by the Commission within three consecutive months of the receipt of the request to prosecute. The Justice Ministry has failed to inform the Commission of the Ministry's decision on the pending cases awaiting indictment, an inaction which the LACC considers as a deliberate attempt by the Ministry to fail the Commission's mandate to coordinate the prosecution of all corruption cases' (p.7).

The 6 October 2014 resignation of the Attorney General of Liberia, Ms Christiana Tah, claiming presidential interferences in the justice system (FrontPage Africa 11/07/2014) further affirms the inaction of the Justice Ministry, and lack of political will to prosecute corruption in Liberia.

Second, the judicial branch of government hinders the prosecution of corrupt cases. For example, the outcome of the only two cases prosecuted by the LACC since its formation remain on the Supreme Court docket. Additionally, the judiciary is corrupt and can therefore not be relied on for prosecuting corruption. According to the US Country Report on Liberia (2013), 'judges are susceptible to bribes to award damages in civil cases, and they request bribes to try cases, release detainees, or to judge defendants not guilty in criminal cases' (p.13). For their part, defence attorneys and prosecutors obtained bribes from defendants to 'secure favourable rulings from the courts or to appease jurors, judges, prosecutors, jurors, and police officers' (US Report 2013, p.13).

Third, a corrupt jury system hinders the general prosecution of corruption in Liberia. For instance, the Bomi County Attorney confirmed that in June 2014 jurors received US$500.00 each, while the bailiff who guarded them equally received US$500.00 as compensation to compromise a case (New Dawn 06/21/2014). The jury's corruption was further attested to by Liberia's former Solicitor General, Michael Wilkins Wrights, who blamed lawyers for corruption among jurors in the justice system (New Dawn 19 June 2012). Also, five jurors investigated for allegedly accepting bribes in a US$1m theft case, were found guilty and sentenced to 90 days imprisonment by presiding Criminal Judge Yusif Kaba (FrontPage Africa 07/16/2012). Ten others were disbanded according to a court ruling. Based on such instances, 'the Ministry of Justice continues its calls to reform the jury system' (US Report 2013, pp.12-13). Can the LACC muster the courage to prosecute cases using a single lawyer in light of such rampant corruption amongst jurors? It is unlikely that the LACC would venture in the prosecution of more corruption cases because corrupt officials have the resources to pay jurors who will in return vindicate the accused officials, hence the dilemma to prosecute or not.

Last, there is an absence of critical complementary legal instruments to enhance the work of the LACC (US Report 2013). For example, the country lacks 'criminal offenses acts based on which the Commission can prosecute, and the Commission also lacks subpoena powers (p.31). In addition to these, the Commission's request and recommendation for the creation of a fast track corruption trial court has fallen on death ears from the legislative and Executive branches of government (LACC Report 2012). Presently, only the 'Criminal Court "C", can prosecute corruption, but this court is already overwhelmed with other criminal cases' (LACC Report 2012, p.31). This indicates that even if corruption cases were speedily being sent to court, the probability of speedy trial remains unlikely. Therefore it can be concluded that the US human rights report on Liberia was correct to state that the law does not 'provide criminal penalties for official corruption, although criminal penalties exist for economic sabotage, mismanagement of funds, and other corruption-related acts; hence officials engaged in corrupt practices with impunity' (US Report 2013, p. 12).

3. POLITICAL BARRIERS

Besides capacity, legal and judicial challenges hindering the LACC's prosecution mandate, the lack of political will is the third major barrier to the effective operation of the Commission. In its 2012 Annual Report, the LACC explicitly states that 'the lack of convincing and demonstrated show of serious commitment to the fight against corruption by all three branches of Government undermines the effectiveness of the Commission' (LACC Report 2012, p. 31). It reports that 'government ministries and agencies do not give maximum support to the Commission during investigations for corrupt acts' (pp.31-32). For instance, the Legislature took 'a total of US$118, 000 in bribery from the National Oil Company for the ratification of the oil reform laws' (FrontPage Africa 2014, 10/02/1014). This bribery claim has been confirmed by the audit conducted by the General Auditing Commission (GAC) of Liberia as well as a former Board Chair of the oil company, Clemenceau Urey, who admitted to a legislative committee that the bribes were paid to fast track oil reform laws ratification (FrontPage Africa 10/02/1014). Additionally, the Legislature and Judiciary have refused to declare assets as required by the Code of Conduct (LACC 2014). They have also failed to succumb to audit by the GAC over the past 11 years (GAC 2013). The National Legislature, and the House Speaker have equally been embroiled in corruption allegations (FrontPage Africa 10/02/14) without appropriate redress.

Furthermore, the National Legislature hinders prosecution of corruption. It deliberately sits on reports of the GAC which has recommended prosecution of public officials accused of abuse, graft and corruption (FrontPage Africa 09/12/14; New Democrat 04/25/2013). The GAC reports to the National Legislature that must clear said reports and submit them to the Executive for appropriate actions. The GAC has presented at least 59 completed reports with some recommending prosecutions to the Legislature, but most of these recommendations have not been passed on for prosecution (PeaceWomen 02/12/14). The LACC could independently use these reports to prosecute, but it lacks the capacity to do so. The Justice Ministry also cannot because it has already defaulted on several other prosecution requests from the LACC.

The Executive for its part has come under series of criticisms for not acting on corruption allegations involving top government officials and political allies of the President. For example, a Canadian investor, Len Lindstrom, out of frustration, published a 618-page book focusing on 'key events, facts and laws pertaining to the case of "Liberty" versus the Ministry of Lands, Mines, and Energy (MLM&E), and the Government of Liberia' (Daily Observer 01/07/2014). His book entitled 'Corruption 101' details his company's (Liberty) fight for justice during 'corruption, extortion, economic sabotage, and violation of court injunctions through bought-off lawyers, tampering with official court records, and repeated flagrant assaults against the Liberian laws' (p. 1). Also, journalist Rodney Sieh was jailed and fined US$1.6m for libel relative to a corruption report against a close confidant of the President, former Agricultural Minister, Dr Chris Toe (Livewire 11/21/2013). Similarly, corruption charges were brought against President Sirleaf, her son and other close allies by the former CEO and President of the National Oil Company of Liberia, Dr Christopher Zeohn Neyor (The Perspective 06/16/2014). Moreover, there have been corruption allegations involving the squandering of millions of US Dollars by relatives, presidential allies and top government officials including 'Robert Sirleaf and Jenny Bernard, the President's son and elder sister, as well as Willie Knuckles, Ms Medina Wesseh, Elva Mitchell Richardson, Lusinee Donzo, Amara Konneh, Harry Greeves', et al. (LIPI 2014 cited in Kaydor 2014, pp.65-68), but no action has been taken on these allegations.

4.   CONCLUSION AND RECOMMENDATIONS

The Liberian Anti-Corruption Commission (LACC) and the Ministry of Justice are responsible for exposing and combating official corruption. The LACC is empowered to prosecute any corruption case, or cases that the ministry declines to prosecute. However, the LACC remains a weak option because of underfunding, understaffing, legal and judicial bottlenecks, and the lack of political will. Liberia's political leaders seem to be comfortable with the feeble anti-corruption laws, poorly staffed and an underfunded anti-corruption commission because their families and allies are linked to allegations of corruption. Similar scenario took place with former Indonesian President Suharto, and Philippines leader Marcos 'who lacked political commitment to eradicate corruption due to their families and cronies' involvement in plundering their countries' (Quah 2003, p. 179). This might also explain why anticorruption laws in Liberia are feeble and selectively implemented, and that the LACC is poorly staffed and underfunded. As Quah (2003) asserts, 'many leaders have adopted "hopeless" strategies that perpetuate corruption instead of stifling it' (p. 176). Liberia finds a place in this expression, and it is therefore arguably right to place it in the "hopeless strategy" quadrant of Jon Quah's (2003) matrix of anti-corruption strategies in Asia (p.179).

Table 1: matrix of anticorruption strategies in Asia

	Adequate anti-corruption measures	**Inadequate anti-corruption measures**
Strong political will	**Effective strategy**	**Ineffective Strategy**
	Singapore and Hong Kong	South Korea
Weak political will	**Ineffective strategy**	**Hopeless strategy**
	Malaysia and Thailand	India, China, Indonesia, Mongolia, Philippines, **LIBERIA**

Source: Quah (2003), Curbing Corruption in Asia, p.179.

Finally, corruption in Liberia, like in Asia, can only be minimized if political leaders are willing to impartially implement effective anticorruption strategies. These include paying civil servants adequate salaries, reducing opportunities for corruption in "wet agencies" by cutting red tape and unnecessary regulation, improving the supervision of civil servants in vulnerable positions, and increasing the probability of detecting and punishing corrupt individuals (Quah 2003). The 'adoption of an independent anti-corruption agency like the LACC to implement anti-corruption measures does not ensure success unless it is accompanied by political will' (p. 178). Success occurs where three conditions are met. These include 'the enactment of comprehensive anti-corruption legislations; an independent anticorruption agency enjoying political will and provided with sufficient personnel and resources to guarantee its independence; and the fair enforcement of the anti-corruption laws by the political system' (p. 177). With these measures in place, the Liberia Anti-Corruption Commission might succeed.

REFERENCES

AllAfrica.com 2014, 'Corruption with impunity: United States 2013 human rights report slams Liberia', *FrontPage Africa* (online edition), 28 February, viewed 2 October 2014, <http://allafrica.com/stories/201402280531.html>.

APEC 2006, *Anti-Corruption and governance: the Philippine experience*, Philippine Institute for Development Studies; Philippines APEC Study Center Network, viewed 1 August 2014, <http://www.apec.org.au/docs/06ascc_hcmc/06_9_1_balboa.pdf>.

FrontPage Africa 2012, 'Tainted and Corrupt Jurors Jailed in Liberia: Five Get 90 Day-Sentence for Bribery', *FrontPage Africa* (online edition), 16 July, viewed 15 August 2014, <http://www.frontpageafricaonline.com/old/news/general-news/3639-jurors-jailed-in-liberia-5-get-90-day-sentence-for-bribery.html>.

_______2014, 'Tyler, NOCAL credibility at stake over 'illegal' payment to lawyers', *FrontPage Africa* (online edition), 2 October, viewed 2 October 2014, <http://www.frontpageafricaonline.com/index.php/news/3223-tyler-nocal-credibility-at-stake-over-illegal-payment-to-lawyers>.

_______2014, 'Liberia: Auditing Commission Submits Audits to Legislature for Action', *FrontPage Africa* (online edition), 12 September, viewed 1 October 2014, <http://allafrica.com/stories/201409121066.html?viewall=1>.

_______2014, 'Distrust, betrayal pushed 'tough skin' Tah out of EJS gov't, *FrontPage Africa* (online edition), 7 October, viewed 8 October 2014, <http://www.frontpageafricaonline.com/index.php/politic/3265-distrust-betrayal-pushed-tough-skin-tah-out-of-ejs-gov-t>.

General Auditing Commission (GAC) 2014, *Audit reports 2008-2012*, Government of Liberia, viewed 5 October 2014,

<http://gacliberia.com/content_list_sub.php?sub=129&related=
26&third=129&pg=sp>.

______Act 2005, Government of Liberia, viewed 5 October 2014,
<http://gacliberia.com/content.php?sub=124&related=1&third
=124&pg=sp>.

Government of New South Wales 2014, 'Prosecution briefs with the DPP
and outcomes, ICAC, New South Wales, viewed 1 October 2014,
<www.icac.nsw.gov.au/investigations/prosecution-briefs-with-the-
dpp-and-outcomes>.

Honk Kong 2014, *ICACA fact sheets, Hong Kong Special Administrative
Region Government,* Information Services Department, Hong Kong,
viewed 20 September 2014, <www.gov.hk/en/about/abouthk/factsheets/
docs/icac.pdf>.

Kaydor, T 2014, *Liberian democracy: a critique of checks and balances,*
Authorhouse, Bloomington, IN, USA.

Kaufmann, D 1997, 'Corruption: The Facts', *Foreign Policy,* no. 107, pp.
114-131.
Kwanue, C 2014, 'Canadian investor releases book on corruption in
Liberia', *Daily Observer* (online edition), 1 July, viewed 2 October 2014,
<http://www.liberianobserver.com/politics/canadian-investor-releases-
book-%E2%80%98corruption%E2%80%99-liberia>.

Larmour, P 2008, 'Corruption and the concept of culture: evidence from
the Pacific Islands', *Crimes Law and Social Change,* vol. 49, pp.225-239.

Liberian 1980 coup d'état, YouTube, viewed 15 August 2014,
<https://www.youtube.com/watch?v=Be2ZdSiJhc0>.

Liberia Anti-Corruption Commission (LACC) Act 2008, Government of
Liberia, viewed 15 August 204,
<http://www.lacc.gov.lr/public/LACC_ACT.pdf>.

_______2012, *2012 Annual Report to President Ellen Johnson Sirleaf*, Government of Liberia, viewed 15 August 2014, <www.lacc.gov.lr/public/ANNUAL%20REPORT%202012-LACC.pdf>.

_______ 2011, 2011 *Annual Report to President Ellen Johnson Sirleaf*, Government of Liberia, viewed 15 August 214, <www.lacc.gov.lr/public/LACC%202011%20ANNUAL%20REPORT. pdf>.

_______2014, 'Legislature and Judiciary', LACC official website, viewed 23 October 2014, <http://www.lacc.gov.lr/public/index.php/about-us/legislature>.

Livewire 2013, 'Three months in hell – Jailed for reporting on corruption in Liberia', *Livewire* (online edition), 21 November, viewed 1 October 2014, <http://livewire.amnesty.org/2013/11/21/three-months-in-hell-jailed-for-reporting-on-corruption-in-liberia/>.

New Democrat 2013, 'Liberia: Legislature ignores GAC report', *New Democrat* (online edition) 25 April, viewed 13 August 2014, <http://allafrica.com/stories/201304251413.html>.

PeaceWomen 2014, 'Liberia: the United Nations Mission in Liberia, facts and figures', *PeaceWomen* (online edition), 12 February, viewed 1 October 2014, <http://www.peacewomen.org/news_article.php?id=4723&type=news>.

Philp, M 1997, 'Defining political corruption', *Political Studies*, vol. 45, pp.436-462.

Quah, J 2003, *Curbing corruption in Asia*, Eastern Universities Press, Singapore.

The Perspective 2014, 'Open letter to President Ellen Johnson Sirleaf', *The Perspective* (online edition), 16 June, viewed 20 August 2014, <http://www.theperspective.org/2014/0616201402.php>.

The New Dawn 2014, 'Liberia: Mercenaries' Lawyer Claims Bribery', *The New Dawn* (online edition), 20 June, viewed 29 September 2014, <http://allafrica.com/stories/201406200898.html>.

The New Dawn 2012, 'Lawyers indicted for bribery', *The New Dawn* (online edition), 19 June, viewed 29 September 2014, <http://thenewdawnliberia.com/index.php?option=com_content&view=article&id=6181:lawyers-indicted-for-bribery&catid=25:politics&Itemid=59>.

Transparency International 2014, *Definition of corruption*, TI, viewed 6 October 2014, <http://www.transparency.org/whatwedo?gclid=CjwKEAjw-8ihBRD2t9qT3NaW7igSJAD3_sNVpJurV8OsaqarRuhO1fY1vmvzXZeamiew1YMQHh--uhoCSJ_w_wcB>.

______2013, Global Corruption Barometer 2013, TI, viewed 6 October 2014, <http://www.transparency.org/gcb2013/country/?country=liberia>.

United States Government 2014, US Bureau of Democracy, *Human Rights and Labor 2013, Country reports on human rights practices 2013*, US Government, viewed 1 October 2014, <http://www.state.gov/documents/organization/220339.pdf>.

United Nations 2004, *UN handbook on practical anti-corruption measures for prosecutors and investigators,* United Nations, NY, viewed 12 August 2014, <http://www.unodc.org/pdf/crime/corruption/Handbook.pdf>.

United Nations 2003, *The United Nations Convention against Corruption (UNCAC) 2003,* United Nations Office on Drugs and Crimes, United Nations, viewed 5 October 2014, <http://www.unodc.org/documents/treaties/UNCAC/Publications/Convention/08-50026_E.pdf>.

United States State Department 2003, *Liberia: 1989-1997 Civil War, Post-War developments, and U.S. relations*, Congress Research Service (CRS) Report, updated 31 December 2003, Nicolas Cook, Foreign Affairs, Defense, and Trade Division, Library of Congress, USA, viewed 1 October 2014,
<http://digital.library.unt.edu/ark:/67531/metacrs8431/m1/1/high_res_d/ RL30933_2003Dec31.pdf>.

Zahiid, S 2013, 'MACC: Malaysia now better than Hong Kong in graft fight', *Malaymail* (online edition), 6 November, viewed 20 September 2014,
<www.themalaymailonline.com/malaysia/article/macc-malaysia-now-better-than-hong-kong-in-graft-fight>.

Thomas Kaydor, Jr.

Sydney Airport Corruption Case

1. Definitions of corruption in the case

In the case, the then Integrity Commissioner, Philip Moss, clearly defines corruption as an abuse of office, offering a bribe to a Commonwealth public official, and receiving a bribe as well as conspiracy to import a commercial quantity of border-controlled precursors' (ACLEI Report 2013, p. 3). Additionally, he reports that 'an officer of the Department of Agriculture, Fisheries and Forestry (DAFF) was arrested and tried for abuse of public office, prohibited disclosure of official information, receiving a corrupting benefit and influencing a Commonwealth public official' (ACLEI Report 2013, p. 3). This adds official information disclosure without authorization to the definition of corruption in the case. The definitions suggest that the abuse of public office, bribery, importation of controlled substances, and unauthorized release of official information, among others, constitute acts of corruption based on the laws of Australia. These acts fall within the legal definition provided in the Fraud and Corruption Control Plan 2014-2015 of the Australia Commission for Law Enforcement Integrity (ACLEI) responsible for preventing, detecting and investigating serious and systematic corruption in six government entities (ACLEI 2014).

The ACLEI defines fraud as dishonestly obtaining a benefit, or causing a loss, by deception or other means. The fraud must be deliberate, not accidental, and may lead to a direct or indirect advantage to an individual or group (Commonwealth Fraud Control Guidelines 2011); and it defines corruption as an 'engagement in conduct that involves an abuse of office, and perverts the course of justice (LEIC Act 2006). In view of these, I agree with the definitions in the case because they cover what fraud and corruption means in my view. All actors in the case agreed with these definitions as there is no evidence of an opposing view to them.

2. CAUSES AND EXPLANATIONS FOR CORRUPTION IN THE CASE

The corruption at the Sydney International Airport resulted from 'a weak integrity culture and changes in the risk environment' (ACLEI Report 2013, p.6). According to the participants, it was widely assumed that there was no corruption at the airport due to lack of evidence. Attention was not focused on systemic vulnerabilities that emerged in the airport integrity systems. Accordingly, when staff who normally would have been involved in 'real-time targeting' were frequently diverted at peak times to perform passenger facilitation roles, no one alarmed.

Additionally, Customs and Border Protection officers adopted what the report refers to as a 'whole of airport strategy', a practice that relocated highly specialized interdiction teams, and allowed staff to carry out widespread tasks. Under such environment, the criminal conspirators gained access to sensitive databases, and engaged in broader sharing of sensitive information and intelligence, thereby increasing the opportunity for corrupt conduct and strategic coordination with criminals. For example, in paragraph 39 (b) of the report, these corrupt officials had information about what flights or which passengers were scheduled for law enforcement scrutiny thereby allowing a drug courier to plan flights and arrival times to avoid detection. In some cases, criminals abandoned baggage containing drugs, if an interdiction were planned after the courier boarded a flight, et al. Insider knowledge about limitations in detection methods meant that drug couriers could be chosen carefully and coached well in advance on methods ensuring that contraband was more difficult for law enforcement officials to detect and locate.

Furthermore, breakdown in effective supervision, noncompliance with the airport standards, and lack of confidence amongst staff also caused the corruption at the Sydney Airport. I think these reasons are convincing, though the acts could have been prevented. It is likely that some high-level officers formed part of the syndicate and therefore decided to adopt hands off approach, which allowed junior officers to carry out the corrupt deals without any punishment. Had there not been the involvement of senior officials, I believe some precautionary measures could have been taken to remedy these problems. For example, incentives could have been provided to whistle blowers for reporting corrupt behaviour at the airport, and corrupt officials could have been punished by the Custom and Border Security department without the intervention of the ACLEI. Without high level knowledge about the corruption, the corrupt syndicate could not have survived for six years.

3.   MEASURING CORRUPTION IN THE CASE

Given the duration of the corruption (2007 to 2013) and the number of officials involved, I think the measurement of the corruption in this case has been underestimated. For example, the report indicates that '54 kilograms of pseudoephedrine were seized, and cash with assets approximately valued at $237,000 confiscated' (LECEI Report 2013, p.3). It mentions instances in which Custom and Border Protection officers aided money laundry by providing safe passage to individuals with huge sums of monies. The officers received bribes for such actions, and built networks with criminal gangs in communities, schools, and 'organized crime groups like the outlawed motorcycle gangs' (p.8) to run illegal deals. Hence, corruption in this case must have been widespread. Various Custom and Border Protection officers got indoctrinated into the corrupt behaviour to the extent that they used 'friends and relatives to facilitate corruption' (ACLEI Report 2013, p.9). It is very difficult to determine in quantitative terms how much corruption must have occurred. The monetary value provided in the report is simply based on tangible cash and some assets seized; hence it appears to be unreliable in terms of the actual monetary value of the corruption in six years.

4.   ANTI-CORRUPTION IN THE CASE

Several anti-corruption measures have been adopted in this case. First, there were arrests, detentions and prosecutions. For instance, four Customs and Border Protection officers got arrested, and one pleaded guilty. Also, 'an officer from the DAFF Border Compliance Division was arrested' (ACLEI Report 2013, p.2). These arrests sent signals that anyone could have been arrested and prosecuted for similar crimes. This must have limited the level of corruption at the Sydney Airport. Second, the report recommended preventive measures to curb corruption in the system. For instance, substantive changes were made in the Custom and Border Protection's integrity policy, practice and organizational arrangements. Additionally, the Parliament, based on recommendations from the ACLEI, enacted the Law Enforcement Integrity Legislation Amendment Act 2012 (LEILA Act 2014). This Act introduced particular anti-corruption measures for Customs and Border Protection officers. These measures include drug and alcohol testing, empowerment of the CEO to dismiss corrupt officers for reason of serious misconduct (this modified appeal rights), and an authority to issue binding orders relating to conduct and integrity (such as mandatory reporting of misconduct, et al.). Also, a corruption vulnerabilities assessment was conducted at the airport. The assessment report proposed strategic changes in the operating procedures and rules at the airport (see p.405 of the report). These measures synchronized Customs and Border Protection officers' power into closer alignment with integrity arrangements.

Third, the Australian Federal Police's support to the investigation increased the expertise of the Australian Crime Commission in investigating the corrupt practices at the Sydney International Airport. Without such support, the investigation process could have taken a longer time, and this might have compromised some investigations along the way. Although, corruption at the Sydney Airport must have been reduced because of these anti-corruption measures, the removal of the renowned and experienced criminal investigator, without replacing the managers at the Sydney airport (They Sydney Morning Herald 2012), casts more doubts over a comprehensive fight against airport corruption in the case. One cannot be certain that the airport manages were not beneficiaries of the corruption. Therefore, a comprehensive reshuffle of the airport managers as well as Customs and Border Protection officers could have consolidated long term anti-corruption measures.

5. INDEPENDENT AGENCIES IN THE CASE

The 'independence' of the ACLEI allowed objective investigation processes. The ACLEI evoked its rights to obtain warrants under the

Surveillance Devices Act 2004, and the Telecommunications (Interception and Access) Act of 1979 to covertly get evidence that it could not have otherwise obtained. The independent agencies also brought credibility to the investigation process because the accused agencies couldn't have led the prolonged surveillance, investigation, arrests and prosecution processes. The ACLEI's briefings and reports to the Parliamentary Committee provided the basis for the enactment of further anti-corruption laws, and led to the inclusion, on 1 July 2013, of three additional government agencies under the supervision of the Integrity Commissioner's jurisdiction (ACLEI Report 2013). The three additional agencies are the Australian Transaction Reports and Analysis Centre (AUSTRAC), the CrimTrac Agency, and prescribed aspects of the Department of Agriculture (ACLEI 2014).

The impact of the independent anti-corruption agency in Sydney Airport Corruption Case is crisply summarised in the statement of the Justice Minister who stated in his farewell statement during Mr Ross' end of tenure, as follows:

> 'as Integrity Commissioner, Mr Moss has provided invaluable leadership in the fight against corruption. He has led a number of significant anti-corruption investigations, including Operation Heritage, which concerned corrupt conduct at Sydney International Airport. These investigations have resulted in strengthened anti-corruption arrangements in Australia's law enforcement and border environments and have been central to maintaining the integrity of Australian law enforcement agencies. Due to his efforts, the Commonwealth now has a well-established and effective law enforcement anti-corruption agency.' (Minster Announcement 21/07/2014)

6. EVALUATION IN THE CASE

Commissioner Philip Moss' interim report on Operation Heritage, in my view, is quite fair and just. It made strategic recommendations some of which led to the enactment of new anti-corruption laws to enhance integrity and reduce corruption amongst government's integrity institutions. Although there are some confidential components of the report that were only provided to the Minister and the Parliamentary Committee, the Minister's farewell statement as well as the new procedures and measures put in place attest to the frantic efforts made to address corruption at the Sydney Airport. These anti-corruption measures must have gone a long way in curbing the scale of corruption that was ongoing. I believe it would be appropriate were the new Integrity Commissioner, Mr Robert Cornall AO, to review the impact of those recommendations in order to gain insights in current corruption trends at the Sydney Airport.

The continuous evaluation of the impacts of the recommendations, and the new laws and procedures would be in fulfilment of Philip Moss' concluding statement in the report. He concludes that

> 'an enduring lesson is that corruption risk will follow opportunity for illicit profit. Policy designers, and those responsible for governance of high-risk operating environments, must expect this situation to be the case, and plan accordingly.' (ACLEI Report 2013, p. 10)

In view of this caveat, the anti-corruption and integrity institutions should not sit back on grounds that corruption has been prevented at the Sydney Airport. It could be that new corruption dynamics are emerging, hence there is a need for continuous engagement amongst various stakeholder in an attempt to stamp out corruption in that sector.

7. READINGS AND THE CASE

Mark Philip's (1997) definition of political corruption agrees with the definitions of corruption at the Sydney Airport. The article defines 'political corruption is a behaviour which deviates from official or public duties in pursuit of private benefits' (Ney 1989 cited in Philp 1997, p. 440). It includes bribery, fraud, electoral malpractice and bribes to parliamentarians. The article also places nepotism under the definition of corruption, something which is quite new to me. Previously, I thought nepotism was not an act of corruption. However, given the scenario from Nick Greiner's case, corruption is not only about pecuniary gains; it is equally an abuse of power or office. In Liberia, most newly appointed and elected government officials normally take along relatives and friends in their offices without being considered corrupt. However, such practice amounts to political corruption. Article five (c) of the Liberian Constitution (1986) forbids nepotism, but the irony is that this constitutional provision is often violated without any penalties.

Furthermore Philp (1997) includes lobby activities within the domain of corruption, something I had previously thought was a legal practice. For instance, the Liberian Legislature receives lobby fees, to enact certain bills and laws, but given that lobby fees are meant for the personal gains of legislators, I am now convinced that they induce legislative actions that would have otherwise not been carried out. Hence whether the outcomes of lobby fees undermine or promote public interest, such inducement is a corrupt practice because lawmakers are paid to do their job and should therefore not receive extra payments to induce them (p.441). Lobbying also links with the practice of businesses and investors using 'an extra-legal institutional framework to gain influence over the actions of the bureaucracy' (Philp 1997, p.444). This aspect of corruption seeks to challenge deeply rooted practices more often than not thought to be a way of life in some societies. This concept of institutional corruption therefore suggests that not all institutional cultures serve the public interest. Hence, the definition of institutional corruption, in my view, brings the integrity of most institutions into question because they sometime engage in practices considered 'culturally acceptable', but which undermine the general interest of the public by promoting the aspirations of certain individuals or groups.

Peter Larmour's (2008) groundbreaking article on corruption and the concept of culture, which provides some evidence from the Pacific Islands, is also relevant to the Sydney Airport case. Three key issues interest me in this article. First, culture tends to accept and justify certain corrupt practices as normal behaviour. For example, gifts from politicians, favours for voters, appointment of relatives, friends and campaign managers (p.236) are all considered normal practices in most societies; yet these acts promote selfish gains as opposed to the community interest. However, the question is when do we draw a line between what is corrupt and what is not, especially considering cultural diversity around the world? Gifts, favours, et al. could be based on good intentions, though they could equally be ill intentioned. Cultural relativism therefore complicates the meaning of corruption and militates against how corruption can be measured. For instance, it is legal to give a token valued at not more than US$200.00 to a Liberian official (Liberia's Code of Conduct 2014, p. 2), whereas this is illegal in Australia. This scenario builds a strong link between culture and ethics; hence the need to be careful when 'trying to understand people's view and response to corruption' (Larmour 2008, p. 237).

Second, the lack of interest in reporting corruption, as highlighted in the Sydney Airport case, seems to cut across countries. In the case of Palau and Tonga, close relationships prevent reporting of corrupt officials (p.232). However, the refusal or failure to report corrupt officials promotes corruption. In the Sydney Airport case, some officials knew about corrupt conduct, but did not report because they saw no benefit in reporting. Failure to report therefore aided corruption at the airport. Consequently, it would be good to create confidential reporting mechanisms for whistle blowers. One of the ways to encourage reporting is the provision of incentives to whistle blowers. This would strengthen the fight against corruption.

Third, bribes are used to sway people's intention to act illegally (Larmour 2008). However, it is mostly the receivers of bribes that are accused of corruption. Therefore, both givers and receivers of bribes should be guilty of corruption because without a bribe giver, there would be no recipient, and vice versa. Finally, it is normally assumed that minimum corruption is better' (Philp 1997, p459), and that corruption is a game of the powerful (Larmour 2008). However, both low and high levels corruption are crimes. Hence all those involved in corruption must be reprimanded. This will help to curb or illuminate corruption. Where moderate corruption is tolerated, it inevitably produces widespread corruption (Larmour 2008); hence no amount of corruption warrants justification.

REFERENCES

Australian Government 2014, Australian Commission for Law Enforcement Integrity (ACLEI) Report *(2013)*, Australian Government, viewed 9 August 2014,
<http://www.aclei.gov.au/Pages/Reports-submissions-and-speeches.aspx>.

ACLEI Website viewed 10 August 2014,
<http://www.aclei.gov.au/Pages/default.aspx>.

Australian Government, *Australian Government Commonwealth Fraud Control Guidelines (2011)*, Australian Government, viewed 10 August 2014,
<http://www.ag.gov.au/Publications/Documents/Commonwealth FraudControlGuidelinesMay2002/Commonwealth%20Fraud%20 Control%20Guidelines%20March%202011.pdf>.

Australian Government 2006, *Australian Law Enforcement Integrity Commissioner Act (2006)*, Government of Australia.

Australian Commission for Law Enforcement Integrity 2014, *Fraud and Corruption Control Plan 2014-2015 of the Australia Commission for Law Enforcement Integrity (ACLEI)*, Australian Government, viewed 23 August 2014,
<http://www.aclei.gov.au/Documents/Accountability/ACLEIfraud andcorruptioncontrolplan201415.pdf>.

Baker, R, Massola, J, McKenzie, N 2014, 'Brother of customs boss to be sentenced', 10 June 2014, *The Sydney Morning Herald*, p. 1.

Constitution of Liberia 1986, viewed 22 August 2014,
<http://www.tlcafrica.com/constitution-1986.htm>.

Government of Liberia 2014, *Code of Conduct (2014)*, Republic of Liberia, viewed 20 August 2014,

<http://www.emansion.gov.lr/doc/Act_Legislature_Prescribing_A_National_Code%20of_Conduct%20(Final_Version%202014).pdf>.

Larmour, P 2008, 'Corruption and the concept of culture: evidence from the Pacific Islands', *Crimes Law and Social Change*, vol. 49, pp.225-239.

Philp, M 1997, 'Defining political corruption', *Political Studies*, vol. 45, pp.436-462.

Minister Announcement 21 July 2014, viewed 15 August 214 <http://www.ministerjustice.gov.au/Mediareleases/Pages/2014/ThirdQuarter/21July2014AustralianCommissionforLawEnforcement IntegrityIntegrityCommissionerendofterm.aspx>.

PART III

INSTITUTIONS AND POLICY PROCESSES

LIBERIA TRUTH AND RECONCILIATION COMMISSION (TRC) RECOMMENDATION 12

1. INTRODUCTION

This essay examines the policy implementation capabilities of Liberia's macro political institutions regarding recommendation 12 in the Liberia TRC report (2009, p.348). It explains why this policy recommendation has not been implemented. The essay provides answers to why changes in 'programmatic and political agenda' (Marsh & McConnell 2010, p.571), and the application of veto powers in a unitary presidential system (Rockman & Weaver 1993) hindered implementation of recommendation 12 between 2009 and 2014. It argues that the change of political interest and programme agenda combined with the presence of veto players impede government's policy implementation capabilities. The research is organized into six parts including this introduction, a review of relevant literature, and brief background of the case. It then presents the research findings, a discussion on why the case unfolded the way it did and concludes with a synthesis of the research outcomes.

2. LITERATURE REVIEW

In 'towards a framework for establishing policy success', Marsh and McConnell (2010) argue that 'there is no systematic criteria to assess policy success' (p.565), but rather 'different groups may assess success or failure based on power relations, competing values and interests' (p.567). They propose a framework for policy assessment. First, any policy success should be measured against a process dimension. This focuses on how policies become legitimate through institutional rules and procedures based on democratic values. Second, the programmatic dimension concentrates on 'the achievement of policy objectives and intended outcomes, the efficient use of available resources, and an assessment of whose interest a policy benefits' (p.571). Last, policy success or failure should be measured by its political outcome. The political aspect examines whether the policy has assisted the government to win an election, get re-elected or accrue legitimacy. A policy may be successful in one or all these dimensions. However, policy success or failure is always contestable because 'political actors and interest groups do not always agree on what constitutes a policy success' (p.575). This makes power relations and interests very important because all policies tend to serve interests. Policy success or failure is therefore relative depending on which interest one represents' (p.575-576).

Marsh and McConnell (2010) assert that the measure of policy failure or success needs to consider unstated policy objectives. It is possible that the stated objectives of a policy might not be the actual intent. This might lead political actors to deviate from the stated objectives of a policy and focus on the unstated objectives which are 'not publicly articulated for fear of being against the public interest' (p.580). Time, space and culture need to also be considered when assessing policy success. A 'policy that appears successful within a short time frame, may seem less successful in the long run' (P. 576). Timing is fundamental because 'governments tend to use shorter timeframes to maximize immediate political and electoral gains' (p.577). In terms of space and culture, 'different political systems have their own culture, values, and socio-economic conditions' (p.577). Therefore, what is regarded as successful in one political system may be considered unsuccessful in another.

Bovens et al. (2006) argue in 'the politics of policy evaluation' that policy evaluation is both a normative and political judgment' (p.319). Accordingly, policy evaluation, in the ideal world, 'is a tool for feedback, learning and improvement; however, in the real world of politics, it becomes a blame game that obstructs rather than enhances the search for better outcomes' (p.320). This affirms Clausewitz's (2006) assertion that 'the politics of policy do not end at policy decision and implementation stages' (p.321). Once adopted, policies migrate from the main public agenda where political choices are made to the less visible arenas of policy implementation where circumstances usually change. Policy evaluation is therefore 'nothing but the continuation of politics by other means' (Bovens et al. p.321). Additionally, once a policy is viewed as a failure, questions about responsibility and liability arise to shift blame. Due to this blame and responsibility threat, 'actors and interests involved in a policy debate engage in blame shifting or damage control' (p.322). Political actors and interest groups will therefore attempt to produce facts and images that suit their interests.

Bovens et al. (2006) divide policy evaluation into two traditions. First the rationalistic tradition emphasizes value neutrality and objective assessment of policy performance. It tries to safe evaluation from the political pressures. Second, the argumentative tradition sees policy evaluation as a process of an informed debate among competing interests and therefore explicitly incorporates politics in its analysis. Despite the difference, policy evaluation 'should rate policies by the degree to which they achieve their stated objectives' (p.329). However, sometimes policy goals are 'unclear or unstated in policy documents, mutually contradictory, or change overtime' (pp.329-330). This makes it difficult to assess policy success based on stated goals only.

In addition to these arguments, institutional veto points can be used as tools to hinder policy implementation and legitimize government's inaction to implement a policy. The 'separation of powers disperses authority among competing political actors through veto points' (Rockman & Weaver 1993, P. 1). These vetoes are used to block or hinder policy implementation once actors' interest and ideas conflict with agreed policy goals. Checks-and-balances prevent a government from 'speaking with a unanimous voice' (p. 2), and spreads blames for policy failures amongst different actors

(Howlett et al. 2009). The separate elections of the Chief Executive and the legislators also balance power as none can remove the other except through an impeachment for certain crimes constitutionally spelt out (Rockman & Weaver 1993). Legislators vote freely on issues based on their political interest. Even with a unity government in which the ruling party gets majority legislative members, 'sanctions for party disciplines are weak because the political interest of legislators is dictated by constituency concerns which override partisan loyalties' (Howlett et al. 2009, p. 60). Additionally, the 'Judiciary can exercise judicial review' (Rockman & Weaver 1993, p.26). This sometimes blocks policy formulation or implementation.

Drawing on these views, it is arguable that after the adoption of policies, the politics continues at the implementation and evaluation stages. Policy goals and objectives also shift over time based on programmatic priorities and political interests. Various actors and interest groups therefore appraise policies based on their interest rather than on objective reality. Moreover, policy failure and success can occur simultaneously depending which dimension is being assessed; hence the difficulty to really prove whether a policy has entirely failed or succeeded. In the case of recommendation 12, institutional veto points have been used as tools to hinder implementation. Veto players have helped to block implementation of recommendation 12.

3. BACKGROUND

On 18 September 2003, Liberia's warring factions signed a peace agreement that ended the country's 14 years civil conflict (CPA 2013). The conflict killed at least 250,000 persons, displaced over 800,000 others, and destroyed basic infrastructure (UN Liberia 2013). Article XIII of the Comprehensive Peace Agreement (CPA) called for the establishment of the TRC to 'investigate heinous crimes and gross human rights violations committed during the war, address issues of impunity and the root causes of the conflict, and facilitate national reconciliation' (CPA 2003, p.11). Amnesty International (2006) defines truth commissions as 'official, temporary, non-judicial fact-finding bodies that investigate a pattern of abuses of human rights and humanitarian law, usually committed over several years' (p.5). Recommendation 12 of the Liberia TRC Report (2009) calls for 'the creation of an extraordinary criminal court to prosecute leaders of warring factions and former rebel fighters considered the most notorious perpetrators of crimes against humanity in Liberia' (pp.349-352).

Besides recommendation 12, 'TRC recommendation 14 barred Liberia's current president, Ms. Ellen Johnson Sirleaf, and 48 persons from public office for 30 years due to their role in the civil war' (TRC 2009, p.361; Aning & Jaye 2011, p.2). However, those affected challenged recommendation 14 at the Supreme Court on grounds that they have the constitutional right to hold political offices. The Court ruled in their favor declaring the political sanction unconstitutional (Schabas 2011). Therefore, Madam Sirleaf and some of those banned from politics contested the 2011 presidential and general elections and won their respective positions. Since then, the government has opted to pursue recommendation 15 which calls for national "palava hut" programme. The "palava hut" programme is a traditional form of conflict resolution and reconciliation through which traditional leaders help to resolve conflicts at community and grassroots levels (TRC Report 2009). It 'affords anyone who commits a crime against an individual or the state, to admit the wrongful act and seek pardon from the people of Liberia' (p.365).

The government has also framed recommendation 12 as a recipe for renewed civil conflict. This negative image (Kingdon 2010) contradicts section 48, Article X of the TRC Act (2005) which mandates that 'all TRC recommendations are authoritative, binding and have the weight of law serving as quasi-judicial directives that must be implemented by the Government of Liberia and National Legislature (Amnesty International 2006, p. 79, Aning & Jaye 2011, pp.5-6). However, there are legal arguments that the recommendations of a truth commission should never be binding on a government because such a requirement contravenes the separation of powers doctrine (Goodfriend et al. 2010).

4. FINDINGS

This research has found out that the Liberian government has not implemented recommendation 12 of the TRC Report (2009) because of two main reasons. First, the political interest and programme agenda have changed over time. For instance, former TRC Commissioner, Pearl

Brown Bull, and some interest groups have framed recommendation 12 as a recipe for future civil conflict in Liberia (Goodfriend et al., pp.10-11). The government has therefore officially endorsed national reconciliation through the "palava hut" programme (Sirleaf 2014) to reconcile the people. National reconstruction, peace and development have become government's primary programme priorities, replacing prosecution and other recommended sanctions. This might have been one of the factors that increased President Sirleaf's popularity as evidenced by a 90.7 per cent popular vote for her reelection in 2011 (NEC 2011). Such popular vote constitutes a political success for the ruling establishment (Marsh & McConnell 2010).

Second, veto points held by the three separate branches of government under the principle of separation of powers in Article three of the Liberian Constitution (1986) were used as a tool to block the establishment of the extraordinary criminal court. The National Legislature could not galvanize a two-third majority to enact the court because individuals and legislators listed for prosecution as well as interest groups against the TRC recommendations lobbied to block passage of any law seeking to establish a war crimes court in Liberia (Goodfriend et al 2010, pp. 10-11). Alternatively, the National Legislature passed a joint resolution to block implementation of the TRC recommendations (p.29). The Supreme Court, for its part, overturned recommendation 14 regarding political sanctions (IPU 2011). Simultaneously, former warring factions, and some interest groups challenged the constitutionality of all TRC recommendations at a Civil Law Court (Goodfriend et al. 2010; Aning & Jaye 2011, pp.14-15). For its part, the Executive prefers a national "palava hut" programme rather than prosecution. It has requested the Law Reform Commission and Justice Ministry to 'review the legal implications of all TRC recommendations (pp.11-12).

These factors combined have hindered the implementation of recommendation 12. Therefore, it can be argued that political systems are designed to promote the interest of political actors under the precepts of 'bounded rationality whereby decision makers use their own decision-making criteria at a time to satisfy their personal interest' (Simon 1955, 1957b cited in Howlett et al., pp.145-146). This further affirms that 'policies serve particular interests, and that policy success is relative depending on which interest one represents' (Marsh and McConnell 2010, p.575).

5. DISCUSSION

Marsh and McConnell (2010) propose three dimensions of policy success or failure. They are 'process, programme and politics' (pp. 572-575). First, the process refers to the 'the policy-making stages through which issues emerge and are framed, options are explored, interests are consulted, and the policy decisions made' (p.572). Under the process dimension, a policy is successful once it passes through constitutional or quasi-constitutional procedures that confer a large degree of legitimacy on the policy outcomes. Applying this to recommendation 12, the TRC Act (2005) was approved by the Liberia National Legislature on 10 June 2005, and signed by the Executive because of a long consultative process between the government and interest groups under the aegis of the United Nations Mission in Liberia (UNMIL), and the United Nations Development Program (Amnesty International 2006). This consultation process was an effort to ensure 'the participation and inclusion of interest groups in the development of the legislation establishing a truth commission modelled after South Africa' (Aning & Jaye 2011, p.7). The Commission was officially launched in June 2006 and completed its work in June 2009 after which it was officially dissolved (TRC Report 2009). The TRC process was therefore successful.

Second, the programmatic dimension concentrates on 'the interests, operational, outcome, and resource aspects of policies' (Marsh & McConnell 2010, p.571). It seeks to answer the following questions. Was the policy 'implemented as per the objectives? Did it achieve the intended outcomes? Was it efficient in the use of available resources, and whose interest did the policy benefit' (p.571)? A policy is also said to be programmatically successful if it reflects the interests of a powerful coalition (p.572). It the case of recommendation 12, non-implementation protects the interest of the ruling elites, former warlords and rebel fighters, and interest groups opposed to a war crimes court in Liberia. However, other actors and interest groups believe that the government has failed to implement recommendation 12, and must therefore resign (Aning & Jaye

2011, pp. 10-11; NDC 2014). This is 'a normative and political judgment' (Bovens et al. p.319).

For the government, recommendation 12 has been reframed thereby focusing attention on the 'national "palava hut" programme, reconstruction and development as the new policy goals on which scarce national resources are being spent' (Sirleaf 2014, p.36). Government argues that spending on national reconciliation, reconstruction and the provision of basic services is more important than spending on war crimes court and prosecution processes (Sirleaf 2014). Furthermore, the government uses recommendation 15 which calls for a 'national "palava hut" programme' (TRC Report 2009, pp. 363-367) to defeat the stated intent of recommendation 12. These two policy recommendations are mutually contradictory and present government with an option to pursue either one or both (Bovens et al. 2006).

Although the stated objectives of recommendation 12 is to prosecute alleged war criminals (TRC Report 2009), the unstated objectives seem to have been the use of the Truth Commission to neutralize tensions from the civil war, provide a space for national reflection, delay prosecution, and entrench the ruling elites in power (Marsh &McConnell 2010). This confirms claims by Howlett et al. (2009) that 'governments often employ temporary bodies or commissions to gather information and procrastinate decision making, hoping that public pressure for action will fade by the time a report emerges' (p.118). Therefore, the TRC has succeeded in the short and medium term because Liberia has been stable and peaceful for the past 11 years despite the absence of the recommended war crimes court. This validates claims by Bovens and t'Hart (1996) that the 'absence of a fixed criteria for success and failure, regardless of time and place, is a serious challenge for determining whether a policy has entirely failed or succeeded (p.4).

Third, policy success or failure should be based on its political outcome. Such measure must examine whether the policy has assisted the government to secure an election victory or increased government's legitimacy and popularity (Marsh & McConnell 2010). The Liberian government's focus on the "palava hut" programme has won it the desired political dividends. The government overwhelmingly got reelected, indicating popular endorsement by the citizens (Marsh & McConnell

2010). The reelection has entrenched the existing elites and protects all those incriminated under recommendation 12 as well as other parts of the report imposing other sanctions (TRC Report 2009).

Furthermore, the fact that the very government which formed the Truth and Reconciliation Commission blocked implementation of recommendation 12 indicates that policies can become political tools for ruling elites to hang on to power (Marsh & McConnell 2010). This also attests that public policy is a political process in which 'policies and actors become represented and evaluated in the political arena marked by interests, emotions, conflicting ideas and power relations' (Bovens et al. 2006, p.330). Simultaneously, time has played a cardinal role in shifting the political agenda. During and after the Commission's operation, the 'political agenda shifted from prosecution and punishment to reconciliation, peace, unity and development' (Goodfriend et al. 2010, p.11). The passage of time has therefore changed the policy mood to the extent that those calling for the creation of the court are viewed as troublemakers wishing to revive civil conflict in Liberia (p.10). This again indicates that the real intent of the TRC might have been a political compromise to calm things down and restore peace, rather than to prosecute alleged war criminals.

Institutions are 'the formal rules, compliance procedures, and standard operating practices that structure the relationship between individuals in various units of the polity and economy' (Hall 1986, p. 19). They constrain or facilitate certain types of human and organizational behavior (North 1990). Liberia's macro political institutions exercised constitutional veto points as tools to hinder implementation of recommendation 12. The bill seeking the creation of the court has been strangulated at the National Legislature, but 'a joint resolution blocking implementation of the TRC recommendations was passed' (Goodfriend et al. 2010, p.29). The Executive frames prosecution as a recipe for renewed civil conflict. It has endorsed recommendation 15 which calls for a national "palava hut" programme. These actions have shifted government's post conflict policy from retributive to distributive justice. For its part, the Judiciary declared recommendation 14, which sanctioned 49 persons from public office, unconstitutional (Schabas 2011). The Supreme Court has one of its 'Associate Justices, Hon. Kabena Janneh, indicted under recommendation 14' (TRC Report 2009, p.p.359-361). Also, interest groups opposed to the

TRC recommendations have petitioned the Civil Law Court to declare all TRC recommendations unconstitutional (Goodfriend et al. p.11).

6. CONCLUSION

This case teaches five major lessons. First, political actor's interest is important in policy implementation processes because they use institutions to privilege their personal interest over the public interest. For instance, recommendation 12 could have been implemented had the Executive and Legislature enacted the extraordinary criminal court (Liberia Constitution 1986). However, all three branches of government privileged their interest over those demanding prosecution. This underscores the significance of institutions in the policy process because they constrain or facilitate actors' behaviors and actions through rules and procedures (Hall 1986).

Second, the case indicates that the policy implementation capabilities of governments in a unitary presidential system are weak because 'many veto points disperse authority amongst different political actors' (Rockman & Weaver 1993, P. 1). Third, the entire policy process and cycle is 'a continuation of politics and interest protection' (Clausewitz 2006, p.321 cited in Marsh & McConnell 2010, p.569). While opposition parties hold strong views about retributive justice, the government pursues distributive justice as its policy preference. Therefore, all former rebel fighters and those indicted in the Liberia TRC report for prosecution as well as other punishments have been granted a blanket amnesty under the pursuit of a national "palava hut" programme.

Fourth, policy goals are sometimes 'unclear or unstated in policy documents, symbolic, mutually contradictory, and often shift overtime (Bovens et al. pp.329-330). Last, policy evaluation is a 'normative and political judgment' (Bovens et al. 2006, p.319). This means that policy success or failure is 'socially constructed and politically articulated based on ideological persuasions' (Taylor & Balloch 2005, p.1).

REFERENCES

Amnesty International 2006, *Liberia Truth, Justice and Reparation Memorandum on the Truth and Reconciliation Commission Act*, Amnesty International, viewed 30 October 2014, <www.amnesty.org/en/library/asset/AFR34/005/2006/en/3205abe5-d41f-11dd-8743-d305bea2b2c7/afr340052006en.pdf>.

Aning, K, Jaye, T 2011, 'Liberia: a briefing paper on the TRC Report', KAIPTC Briefing Paper, Kofi Annan International Peacekeeping Training Centre, Accra, Ghana, viewed 26 September 2014, <http://www.operationspaix.net/DATA/DOCUMENT/6765~v~Liberia__A_Briefing_Paper_On_The_Truth_and_Reconciliation_Commission_Report.pdf>.

Bovens, M, 't Hart, P 1996, *Understanding policy fiascos*, New Brunswick, NJ, Transaction Press.

Bovens, M. 't Hart, P, Kuipers, S 2006, 'The politics of policy evaluation', in M. Moran, M. Rein, and R,E, Goodin (eds), *The Oxford Handbook of Public Policy*, Oxford University Press, pp.319-35.

Constitution of Liberia 1986, Government of Liberia, viewed 31 August 2014, <http://www.ilo.org/wcmsp5/groups/public/---ed_protect/---protrav/---ilo_aids/documents/legaldocument/wcms_126725.pdf>.

Goodfriend, L, James-Allen, P, Weah, A 2010, 'Liberia: beyond the Truth and
Reconciliation Commission-transitional justice options in Liberia', International Center for Transitional Justice, viewed 26 September 2014, <http://ictj.org/sites/default/files/ICTJ-Liberia-Beyond-TRC-2010-English.pdf>

Hall, P.A. 1986, *Governing the Economy: The Politics of State Intervention in Britain and* France, Oxford University Press, New York, USA.

Howlett, M, Perl, A, Ramesh, M 2009, *Studying public policy: policy cycles and policy subsystems,* 3rd edition, Oxford University Press, Toronto.

International Parliamentary Union (IPU) 2011, *Data for parliamentary chambers, Liberia House of Representatives*, IPU, viewed 27 September 2014, <http://www.ipu.org/parline-e/reports/2183_E.htm>.

Kingdon, J 1995, *Agendas, alternatives and public policies,* 2nd edition, Longman, New York, USA.

Marsh, D, McConnell, A 2010, 'Towards a framework for establishing policy success', *Public Administration*, vol. 88, no. 2, pp.564-83.

National Democratic Coalition (NDC) 2014, 'The need for a new government: National Democratic Coalition (NDC) position on contemporary national issues in Liberia', *FrontPage Africa* (online edition), 14 October, viewed 3 November 2014,
<http://www.frontpageafricaonline.com/index.php/op-ed/commentaries-features/3355-the-need-for-a-new-government-national-democratic-coalition-ndc-position-on-contemporary-national-issues-in-liberia>.

National Elections Commission (NEC) 2011, Liberia: 2011 Presidential and Legislative results, NEC, Government of Liberia, viewed 1 November 2014,
<http://www.necliberia.org/results2011/>.

Rockman, B, Weaver, R 1993, 'Assessing the effects of institutions', in R.K. Weaver and B.A. Rockman (eds.) *Do Institutions Matter? Government Capabilities in the United States and Abroad*, the Brookings Institution, Washington D.C.

Schabas, W 2011, 'Liberian Supreme Court Declares TRC Provisions Unconstitutional', *PhD Studies in Human Rights* (online edition) February 17, viewed 27 September 2014,
<http://humanrightsdoctorate.blogspot.com/2011/02/liberian-supreme-court-declares-trc.html>.

Sirleaf, J 2014, *Consolidating the processes of transformation: annual message to the Third Session of the 53rd National Legislature of the Republic of Liberia*, Government of Liberia, viewed 1 November 2014, <http://www.liberianobserver.com/politics/full-text-president-sirleafs-state-nation-address-national-legislature>.

Taylor, D, Balloch, S 2005, 'The politics of evaluation: an overview', in D. Taylor and S. Balloch (eds), *The Politics of Evaluation: Participation and Policy Implementation*, Bristol: The Policy Press, pp.1-17.

Truth and Reconciliation Commission 2009, *Consolidated final report, Truth and Reconciliation Commission, vol. II, (2009)*, TRC, Republic of Liberia June, viewed 29 September 2014, <http://trcofliberia.org/resources/reports/final/volume-two_layout-1.pdf>.

United Nations in Liberia 2013, *One programme: The UN Development Assistance Framework (UNDAF 2013-2017)*, Monrovia, viewed 14 October 2014, <http://unliberia.org/doc/undaf_doc.pdf>.

United States Institute of Peace 2014, *Accra Comprehensive Peace Agreement (CPA) 2013*, US Institute of Peace: digital collection of peace agreements, viewed 31 August 2014, <http://www.usip.org/sites/default/files/file/resources/collections/peace_agreements/liberia_08182003.pdf>.

LIBERIA DIRECT DISTRICT DEVELOPMENT FUND

1. INTRODUCTION

This essay examines the policy reform capabilities of Liberia's macro political institutions. It explains the application of veto powers in a unitary presidential system (Rockman & Weaver 1993) using the Liberia direct district development fund (Tyler 2014) as a case. The essay provides answers to why the use of veto powers in the Liberian Presidential System hindered government's policy reform capabilities between 2013 and 2014. It argues that the presence of many constitutional veto points within the Liberian Presidential System weakens government's policy reform capabilities. The essay is organized into five parts including this introduction, a review of relevant literature, a brief background of the case, the research findings, a discussion on why the case unfolded the way it did, and a synthesized conclusion.

2. LITERATURE REVIEW

In a presidential system, 'the separation of powers disperses authority among competing political actors through veto points' (Rockman & Weaver 1993, P. 1). These veto points are used to block or hinder policy reform whenever actors' interest and ideas conflict with proposed policy reforms. Checks-and-balances prevent a government from 'speaking with a unanimous voice' (p. 2), hinders effective policymaking, and spreads blames for policy failures amongst different actors (Howlett et al. 2009). The separate elections of the Chief Executive and the legislators also balance power as none can remove the other except through an impeachment for certain crimes spelt out in the constitution (Rockman & Weaver 1993). Legislators vote freely on issues because their election and re-election are based on how best they serve their constituents. Even with a unity government in which the ruling party gets majority legislative members, 'sanctions for party disciplines are weak because the political interest of legislators is dictated by constituency concerns which override partisan loyalties' (Howlett et al. 2009, p. 60). Additionally, the 'Judiciary can exercise judicial review' (Rockman & Weaver 1993, p.26) and can sometimes block policy reforms. Presidential systems may therefore guarantee policy stability and path dependence once a policy is already in place.

Ellen Immergut (1993) examines why institutional dynamism impact political decision making across systems, and why 'enacting laws requires successive affirmative consensus votes at all decision points' (p. 63). She argues that to pass certain laws the executive must get the consent of the legislature by galvanizing the necessary votes. This affirms claims by Howlett et al. (2009) that the 'executive sometimes bargains with legislators, offering them administrative and budgetary concessions in return for support, and thereby changing the original intent of policy proposals' (p.60). Consequently, 'institutional mechanisms place veto points on competing political actors, restrict unlimited choices, and at times allow binding decisions' (Immergut 1993, p.64). This helps to explain how conflicts are resolved in political systems, and why some policy reforms are difficult.

Drawing on these views, it can be argued that the constitution creates institutional veto points that hinder policy reform capabilities under the presidential system in Liberia. For instance, the Constitution of Liberia (1986) grants veto points to the Legislature, Executive and Judiciary. The House of Representatives and the Senate must concur on legislations before the President signs them into law (Article 29). Failure of one of the two to concur with the other stalls a legislation. The President can also veto a legislation passed by the Legislature; however, the legislature can override a presidential veto with a two-thirds majority (Article 35). If the Legislature and the Executive pass a law, the Supreme Court can revoke same under a judicial review (Article 2) based on contestation from any citizen or actors. Interest groups and the public therefore have many access points to influence the exercise of these veto points (Besley & Case 2003 cited in Howlett et al. 2009, p. 60) in Liberia.

3. BACKGROUND

On 4 November 2013, the House of Representatives undertook a nationwide consultation to obtain citizens' views on Liberia's Petroleum

Exploration and Production Act 2013 (Legislative Press Statement 2013). During the consultations, the House Speaker and legislators observed an acute lack of basic services in rural communities. They argued that previous national budgets, containing appropriations for infrastructure including clinics, schools, roads et al. did not significantly impact rural communities; hence they proposed a legislation to allocate US$73m in the 2014/2015 National Budget (Tyler 2014). This proposal, welcomed by some opposition politicians and the general voting public from the 73 electoral constituencies (Sonpon 2014), was opposed by the Senate on grounds that the proposed legislation contravened the Public Financial Management Law of 2009 (Watkins 2014). Other actors also negatively framed the legislation as a campaign tool to elect representatives as Senators in the October 2014 midterm elections, and the Speaker as President in the 2017 presidential elections (Watkins 2014).

4. FINDINGS

This research has found out that the Liberian Presidential system has low reform capabilities because of several veto points held by the three separate branches of government under the principle of separation of powers in Article three of the Liberian Constitution (1986). For example, the direct district development fund legislation was blocked by the Senate. This hindered the policy reform and denied voters in electoral districts direct access to development funds in the 2014/2015 national budget. Based on the policy outcome, it can be argued that political systems are designed to promote the interest of political actors under the precepts of 'bounded rationality whereby decision makers use their own decision-making criteria at a time to satisfy their personal interest' (Simon 1955, 1957b cited in Howlett et al., pp.145-146).

5. DISCUSSION

Institutions are 'the formal rules, compliance procedures, and standard operating practices that structure the relationship between individuals in various units of the polity and economy' (Hall 1986, p. 19). They constrain or facilitate certain types of human and organisational behaviour (North 1990). Liberia's macro political institutions exercised constitutional veto points to constrain a legislation regarding the direct allocation of funds to electoral districts. The Senate and President use their veto points to hinder a legislation unanimously endorsed by the House of Representatives. The Senate applied a veto and blocked the legislation based on recommendations from its Budget Committee, which recommended an increase in the existing County Development Fund (CDF) from US$200,000 to US$1 million for each of the 15 counties' (Watkins 2014). The Senate considered the reform illegal. The Executive also considered the reform to be untimely due to lack of resources, though it welcomed the district development fund concept in principle (Morris 2014). However, the Executive increased the existing County Development Fund to US$18.25 to undertake direct district development projects based on the Public Financial Management Laws and Article 34 (AllAfrica.com 2014). This was an endorsement of the Senate's proposal, but also a weak compromise with the Representatives. Hence, an 'incremental policy reform occurred whereby only marginal adjustment was made to the County Development Fund' (Howlett et al. 2009, p.147) thereby further hindering the passage of reform legislation.

The proposed policy reform did not unfold based on the five stages of policy making. It emerged at the decision-making level whereby the Speaker used the official opening of the 53rd Legislature as a policy window and venue to propose the reform (Kingdon 1995), but veto points by the Senate and the President stalled the reform process. This affirms Kingdon's (1995) claims that 'elected officials play more important role in policymaking, and that proposals which lack political backing are less likely to get on the decision agenda' (pp.201-202). The Speaker, as the policy entrepreneur campaigned for the passage of the legislation and got the unanimous consent of the Representatives (Kingdon 1995). However, the Senate and President negatively framed the image of the legislation by terming it illegal, untimely and unrealistic. The refusal of these two veto holders to accept the policy reform undermined allocation of funds directly to districts for local development projects. However, the lack of political will by the Senate and President blocked the policy reform process.

6. CONCLUSION

This case teaches three key lessons under a unitary presidential system. First, political actor's interest is important in policy reform processes because they use institutions to privilege their personal interest over the public interest. For instance, this reform could have occurred had the Executive and Senate concurred, but they privileged their interest over the Representatives and the constituencies. Second, institutions are important in policy reforms because they constrain actors through rules and procedures; in this case, constitutional vetos stalled the policy reform. Finally, the case proves that the reform capabilities of governments in a unitary presidential system are weak because many veto points disperse authority amongst different political actors (Rockman & Weaver 1993, P. 1).

REFERENCES

AllAfrica.com 2014, Viewed 31 August 2014, 'Liberia: from U.S. $73m to U.S.$18.25m: executive compromises on Legislature's proposed U.S.$73 Million', *AllAfrica.com* (online edition), 5 June, viewed 31 August 2014, <http://allafrica.com/stories/201406050754.html>.

Government of Liberia 2014, *The Constitution of Liberia 1986*, Government of Liberia, viewed 31 August 2014, <http://www.ilo.org/wcmsp5/groups/public/---ed_protect/---protrav/---ilo_aids/documents/legaldocument/wcms_126725.pdf>.

Hall, P.A. 1986, *Governing the Economy: The Politics of State Intervention in Britain and France*, Oxford University Press, New York, USA.

Howlett, M, Perl, A, Ramesh, M 2009, *Studying public policy: policy cycles and policy subsystems*, 3rd edition, Oxford University Press, Toronto.

Immergut, E 1993, 'The rules of the game: the logic of health policy-making in France, Switzerland, and Sweden', in i Sven Steinmo, Kathleen Thelen and Frank Longstreth (eds), *Structuring Politics, Historical Institutionalism in Comparative Analysis*, Cambridge University Press, Cambridge.

Kingdon, J 1995, *Agendas, alternatives and public policies*, 2nd edition, Longman, New York, USA.

Liberia National Legislature 2014, *Legislative Press Statement 1 November 2013*, Liberia National Legislature, Government of Liberia, viewed 31 August 2014, <http://legislature.gov.lr/house/news/2013/11/house-county-tour-proposed-oil-law>.

Morris, K 2014, 'Sirleaf endorses US$18m for district development', *Daily Observer* (online edition), 4 June, viewed 31 August 2014, <http://www.liberianobserver.com/politics/sirleaf-endorses-us18m-district-development>.

North, D 1990, *Institutions, Institutional Change and Economic Performance*, Cambridge University Press, Cambridge.

Rockman, B, Weaver, R 1993, 'Assessing the effects of institutions', in R.K. Weaver and B.A. Rockman (eds.) *Do Institutions Matter? Government Capabilities in the United States and Abroad*, the Brookings Institution, Washington D.C.

Sonpon, L 2014, 'UPP supports us$73m direct district development fund', *Daily Observer* (online edition), 5 February, viewed 31 August 2014, <http://www.liberianobserver.com/news/upp-supports-us73m-direct-district-development-fund>.

Tyler, A 2014, Liberia National Legislature, *Full text of Speaker Alex Tyler address at the formal opening on the 3rd session of the Liberia National Legislature on 13 January 2014*, Government of Liberia, viewed 30 August 2014,
<http://legislature.gov.lr/house/news/2014/1/full-text-speaker-tyler-address-formal-opening-third-session-jan-132014>.

Watkins, S 2014, 'US$73m bill violates PFM Act - Says Senate, but Tyler rejects'
The Independent (online edition), 3 June, viewed 31 August 2014, <http://theindependentliberia.com/index.php/politics/90-headlines/803-us-73m-bill-violates-pfm-act-says-senate-but-tyler-rejects>.

PART IV

NATIONAL AND INTERNATIONAL DEVELOPMENT

MIDDLE INCOME TRAP: THE CASE OF THAILAND

I. INTRODUCTION TO THE CASE

On 1 July 2011, Thailand became a middle-income economy (World Bank 2014). This economic progress translated into poverty reduction, improved wellbeing, and increased access to public goods and services. For example, 'over 40 per cent of the Thai population escaped poverty in the past 25 years' (Jitsuchon 2012, p.13). However, Thailand's national income statistics (1952-2011) show declining annual growth rates from about ten per cent in early 1990s and afterward due to the Asian and global financial crises, the 2011 floods and political instability (World Bank 2014). Since 1997, Thailand's growth rate has stagnated around four per cent (Jitsuchon 2012), and its current GDP per capita is US$4420 (UNDP 2014). Due to this stagnant growth, Thailand is said to be caught in a 'middle income trap' (Benyaapikul & Phongpaichit 2013, p.1). A middle-income trap results 'when a country graduates from a low-income economy to a middle-income economy but stagnates without much prospect of advancing to a developed country status' (Gill et al. 2007 cited in Jitsuchon 2012, p.15, Kharas and Kholi, p.281).

Although there are more complex issues to address to promote growth in Thailand, this essay argues that political instability remains the country's binding constraint. This constraint results from recurrent military interventions in Thai politics, centralized state power, and the failure of key political actors to reach mutually beneficial political compromises (Chambers 2010). The essay therefore proposes that the government of Thailand decentralize power to elected regional governments that will manage local development programmes while the central government concentrates mainly on macro level issues like monetary policy and national security.

II. KEY PROBLEM OR ISSUE IN THE CASE

In 1932, Thailand became a constitutional monarchy, replacing the absolute monarchy that was considered a barrier to Thai development (Dixon 1999). Since then, the country adopted 17 different constitutions, and witnessed over 18 actual and attempted military coups (Tweechie 2011). Thailand is politically unstable because of the recurrent meddling of the military into politics (Chambers 2010). As Laothamatas (1988) contends, bureaucrats and military officers centrally manage the affairs of the state. The country, according to Chambers (2010), is a 'tutelary democracy, 'a form of defective and unstable democracy under which non-elected elites (the monarch, privy council and military) hold veto powers over elected officials' (p.837).

In early 2014, failure of the two major rival parties in Thailand to reach political compromise led to another military intervention. Thousands of protesters led by Suthep Thaugsuban, former deputy prime minister and powerbroker in the Democratic Party ('Yellow Shirts') mainly Southerners locked down Bangkok, forcing Prime Minister Yingluck Shinawatra of the Pheu Thai Party ('Red Shirts' predominantly from the North and Northeast) to step down, despite a confidence vote from parliament (Nehru 2014). Due to the political stalemate and eventual breakdown of law and order resulting from the demonstration amongst rival parties, the Thai military declared martial law on 20 May 2014, ordered the cabinet to report to it, and banned gatherings of more than five people (BBC News 22/05/2014). Thailand is presently under a military dictatorship.

III. THEORETICALLY INFORMED DISCUSSION OF THE PROBLEM

Political instability is Thailand's major challenge. First, it undermines economic growth and development, and weakens the share of investment in GDP (Alesina and Perotti 1996). Empirical studies have tested and agreed with said relationship. For example, studies by Barro et al. (1997) and Barro (1996) show a direct negative impact of political instability on economic growth. Also, political instability is a fundamental variable to explain the systematic underperformance of African countries between 1970 and1990 (Guillaumont et al. 1999, Azam et al. 1996 cited in Kefi & Zouhaier 2011, p.798). For their part, De Haan and Siermann (1996) do not contest the effect of instability on growth, but state that instability negatively impacts investment, and low investment slows growth.

Second, instability stalls the building of effective institutions, one of the deep determinants of growth (Rodrik 2003). Institutions are important for sustainable economic growth, but without stability, such growth remains utopian. Peter Hall (1986) defines institutions as 'the formal rules, compliance procedures, and standard operating practices that structure the relationship between individuals in various units of the polity and economy' (p.938). Institutions provide incentives for investment and structure an economy (North 1991). For instance, the Republic of Botswana grew at 7.7 per cent annually from 1965 to 1998 due to the viable political institutions that guaranteed property rights, law and order, prudent resource management, merit based public bureaucracy, and investment in education, health and infrastructure (Acemoglu et al. 2001 cited in Rodrik 2003).

Third, political instability impedes growth, freedom, and prosperity. Thailand is generally violent, socially divided and overwhelmed by populist movements with a large number of actors capable of blocking reforms (Chambers 2010). These divisive factors prevent the building of democratic institutions like those in Botswana, Japan, South Korean, Singapore, et al (Rodrik 2010). The unstable environment undermines economic growth because Thailand operates as a centralized bureaucratic polity mostly ruled by the military class. In addition to this, 'parties use ministerial positions to enhance factional power in a continuing process of logrolls' (Pasuk &

Baker, 2000, p. 138), and corruption is widespread in the public sector (Pasuk & Baker, 1998, p. 260). Such governance deficiencies are a result of weak institutions nurtured by instability. As Acemoglu and Robinson (2012) argue, authoritarian, centralized and exclusive institutions, like those in Thailand, have disastrous consequences on growth as they avail no incentives for investment and innovation. Accordingly, 'it is politics, not geography, culture, et al., that determines the economy' (p. 544). Effective institutions create a level playing field whereby most citizens can enjoy secure property rights, gain access to an independent judicial system, develop their personal capabilities (North 1991), and invest in technology and innovation for steady economic progress (Jones & Romer 2010). Institutions become even more effective when they are inclusive and decentralized.

Last, instability is further compounded by constitutional biases against elected officials. This increases political volatility. For instance, the constitution allows the military and judiciary to appoint and approve independent bodies, such as the National Counter Corruption Commission, the Election Commission, and the Constitutional Court Judges (Thai Constitution 2007). The military can institute marshal law, and effect promotions in its ranks and file (Chambers 2010). The constitution also forbids the Parliament from approving Thai military budget, which sharply rose from 'US$2b in 2006 to about US$6b in 2011' (Chambers 2010, p.850). It grants 'vetos to the non-elected monarch, privy council and the military' over elected parliamentarians (Chambers 2010, p. 827). Finally, the Thai judiciary sometimes interferes with the parliament by removing prime ministers as was done in 2007, 2008 (Howes & Lopez, 2013, p.8), and 2014 (BBC News 22/05/2014). Such practices increase political instability and slow economic growth in Thailand (Kuhonta 2011).

IV. DECENTRALISATION AS A PATHWAY TO STABILITY AND ECONOMIC GROWTH

Economic reforms are one of the options for growth in Thailand. According to Jitsuchon (2012), Thailand's growth relied on 'cheap labour, and low innovation, with technological acquired mainly through technology importation' (p.15). As one of the stylized facts of growth predicts, once a state grows towards the technology frontier, its growth slows (Jones & Romer 2010). Thus, Thailand's old growth model can no longer expand growth. However, if one should rely on economic growth theory, then the country must readjust its economic model. It must diversify production networks (Kharas & Kholi 2011), break monopolistic powers, decentralize governance, and invest in education, research and development to trigger innovations (Jimanez et al. 2012, Acemoglu & Zillibotti 1999). However, all these growth corridors cannot survive amidst political instability in Thailand (Alesina & Perotti 1996).

Consequently, Thai reform agenda must focus on decentralization to create political stability as a precursor to all other reforms. Decentralisation is the transfer of powers from central government to lower levels in an administrative hierarchy (Crook & Manor 1998). It locally provides efficient public goods compared to central government (Oates 1972). Decentralization creates an enabling environment for inclusive political, economic and social reforms because the locals directly lead decision making; it therefore usually promotes political stability. Decentralization gives local authorities the freedom to compete, innovate, and attract investment and technology, which generate local employment, productivity and growth. Employment opportunities drive skills development through education to enhance human capital (TDRI 2012). Enhanced human capital increases productivity and promotes innovation; and all of these factors combined increase growth (Jones & Romer 2010).

To begin the process of decentralization, the current Thai government should constitutionally set up regional governments. The regional governments will comprise locally elected parliaments, premiers and appointed judiciaries. They will manage and support regional and local development programmes and invest in economic activities like agriculture and industry. The central government would focus on macro level issues like monetary policy and national security. Decentralization might shift attention from Bangkok to regional governments, promote equitable distribution of economic opportunities, increase competition and accountability, enhance trade and investment, and spur innovation. It will stabilize Thailand because the 'Yellow Shirts', mainly Southerners, would focus on their regional government, while the 'Red Shirts' would concentrate on theirs in the North. The military and political elites in

Bangkok would be compelled to address regional demands to gain regional authorities' support.

While decentralization might increase political stability, increase access to basic services, promote regional competition, and spur growth, it might cause new problems such as a clash in resource allocation between the central and local authorities, and the decline of state macroeconomic management. According to Zhong Zhu Ding (1998), decentralization complicates and disturbs China's growth and development. In September 1995, Chinese President Jiang Zemin said 'in the process of structural reform, some provinces favoured their local interests and therefore resisted the central government's policies' (Zhong p.63). Decentralization in Thailand might therefore weaken central macroeconomic management and undermine national unity. However, Thailand needs to constitutionally spell out the powers of central and provincial governments to mitigate against the possible drawbacks of devolution.

REFERENCES

Alesina, A, Perotti, R 1994, 'The political economy of growth: a critical survey of the literature', *The World Bank Economic Review*, no. 8, pp. 351–71.

Acemoglu, D, Robinson, J 2012, *Why nations fail: the origins of power, prosperity and poverty*, New York, USA.

Acemoglu, D, Zillibotti, F 1999, 'Productivity differences', NBER Working Papers No. 6879, National Bureau of Economic Research, Cambridge, MA.

Baker, C, Pasuk, P 1998, *Thailand's boom and bust*, Silkworm Books, Chiang Mai, Thailand.

Barro, J 1996, 'Democracy and growth', *Journal of Economic Growth*, no.1, pp.1-27.

Barro, RJ, 1997, *Determinants of economic growth: A cross–country empirical study*, MIT Press, Cambridge, USA.

BBC World News 2014, viewed 9 August 2014, <http://www.bbc.com/news/world-asia-25149484>.

BBC World News 2014, viewed 15 August 2014, <http://www.bbc.com/news/world-asia-27297478>.

Benyaapikul, P, Phongpaichit, P 2013, *Political economic dimension of a middle-income trap: challenges and opportunities for policy reform in Thailand*, Bangkok, Thailand.

Chambers, P 2010, 'Thailand on the brink: resurgent military, eroded democracy', *Asian Survey*, vol. 50, no. 5, pp. 835-858.

Crook, R, Manor, J 1998, *Democracy and decentralization in South Asia and West Africa*, Cambridge University Press, Cambridge.

De Haan, J, Siermann, J 1998, 'Further evidence on the relationship between economic freedom and economic growth', *Public Choice*, no. 95, pp.363-380, MIT Press, Cambridge.

Dixon, J, Heffernan, M 1991, *Colonialism and development in the contemporary world*, London, England, New York, Mansell Pub.

Dixon, J 1999, *The Thai economy: uneven development internationalization*, New York, Routledge.

Hall, P, Taylor, R 1992, 'Political Science and the three new institutionalisms', *Political Studies*, vol. 44, no.5, pp. 936-957.

Howes, S, Lopez, G 2013, 'Thailand: economic growth achievements and challenges', Crawford 8000 case study, Crawford School of Public Policy, ANU, Canberra, ACT.

Jimenez, E, Nguyen, V & Patrinos, H 2012, Human Development Network Education Unit Policy Research Working Paper 6283, The World Bank, Washington DC, USA.

Jitsuchon, S 2012, *Thailand in a middle-income trap*, Thailand Development Research Institute, Bangkok, viewed 8 August 2014, <http://tdri.or.th/archives/download/quarterly/text/T5J2012002.pdf>.

Jones, I, Romer, M 2010, 'The new Kaldor facts: ideas, institutions, population and human capital', *American Economic Journal: Macroeconomics*, vol. 2, no. 1, pp. 224-245.

Kefi, M, Zouhaier, H 2011, 'Institutions and economic growth', *Asian Economic and Financial Review*, vol. 2, no.7, pp.795-812.

Kharas, H, Kohli, H 2011, 'What is the middle income trap, why do countries fall into it, and how can it be avoided?' *Global Journal of Emerging Market Economies*, vol. 3, No. 3, pp. 281-9.

Kuhonta, E 2011, *The institutional imperative: the politics of equitable development in Southeast Asia*, Stanford University Press.

Laothamatas, A 1988, 'Business and politics in Thailand: new patterns of influence', *Asian Survey*, vol. 28, no. 4, pp.451-470.

Nehru, V 2014, 'There is still a way out in Thailand's crises, The Jakarta Globe (online), 17 January, viewed 13 August 2014 <http://carnegieendowment.org/2014/01/17/there-still-is-way-out-of-thailand-s-crisis>.

North, D 1991, 'Institutions', American Economic Association Stable, *The Journal of Economic Perspectives*, vol. 5, no. 1, pp. 97-112.

Oates, E, 1972, *Fiscal federalism*, New York, USA.

Rodrik, D 2003, 'What do we learn from country narratives?' in Robrik, D (ed), *In Search of prosperity*, Princeton University Press.

Thailand Development Research Institute (TDRI) 2012, *Revamping the Thai Education System: Quality for all*, a collection of research papers for TDRI 2011 year-end conference, Bangkok, Thailand.

Thailand Constitution 2007, viewed 10 August 2014, <https://www.constituteproject.org/constitution/Thailand_2007.pdf>.

The World Bank 2014, viewed 15 August 2014, <http://www.worldbank.org/en/country/thailand/overview>.

Tweedie, P 2011, 'Thailand election primer', *The Asia Foundation*, 29 June, viewed 9 August 2014, <http://asiafoundation.org/in-asia/2011/06/29/thailand-election-primer/>.

UNDP Thailand 2014, viewed 10 August 2014, <http://www.th.undp.org/content/thailand/en/home/ourwork/democraticgovernance/overview.html>.

Zhong, D 1998, 'Decentralization and new central-local conflicts in China', *American Asian Review*, vol. 16 no. 4, pp.63-94.

Thomas Kaydor, Jr.

FINDING A REMEDY TO UNITED STATES (US) INEQUALITY

1. INTRODUCTION

United States' rising income inequality is a fundamental problem (Chetty et al. 2014). It 'gets more people in poverty as the middle class hallows out' (Stiglitz 2014, p.1). US inequality is a combined economic, socio-political and policy issue. This must be addressed because it might have undesired consequences on the society. High levels of inequality might lead to 'depression, drug abuse, alcoholism, criminality and high prison rates, economic and social insecurity, infant mortality, mental illness et al.' (Judt 2010, pp.5-6). Such vices hinder mobility from disadvantage classes to the middle and top classes. This affirms that 'no society can flourish and remain happy while a greater part of its members is poor and miserable' (Smith 1776 cited in Judt 2010, p.5). Therefore, as a democrat on the domestic economic and social policy team of the newly elected US administration, the government's primary policy priority is to reduce income inequality. This will 'increase access to social, economic, and political opportunities' (Bastagli et al. 2012, p. 4).

Low levels of income inequality can be achieved through improved wages for the poor and bottom income earners. This essay therefore argues that government needs to invest in quality education for the poor and bottom income earners. Education will enhance human capital, increase productivity, raise income, lower inequality and expand opportunities (World Bank 2008) for all Americans.

2. KEY ISSUE IN THE CASE

Since 1980, 'the world has been obsessed with wealth creation, privatization and growing disparities between the rich and poor' (Judt 2010, p. 1). The US experiences its share of this disparity and has the highest level of inequality amongst OECD countries (OECD 2014b). For instance, the 'average income of the richest ten per cent in the US is 16 times as large as for the poorest ten per cent' (p.2). Presently, the richest one per cent of Americans accounts for 20 per cent of national pre-tax income (OECD

2014b). Income inequality in America is not the result of 'inexorable laws of economics, but rather of policies' (Stiglitz 2014, p.1) including fiscal, education, health, minimum wage, et al. Income inequality lowers equality of opportunities, and it remains America's binding constraint.

3. THEORETICALLY INFORMED DISCUSSION OF THE ISSUE

Rising US inequality is caused by several factors amongst which are the following. First, corporate avarice increases inequality in America. The income of the middle- and bottom-income earners is diminishing, while that of the top ten per cent is expanding. According to Beck and Gordon (2008), the income of the top ten per cent earners comprising CEOs, superstars, investment bankers and lawyers rose from 27 per cent in 1966 to 45 per cent in 2001. In 2005, 21.2 per cent of America's national income accrued to one per cent top earners. Also, in 2010, Wal-Mart CEO earned '900 times the wages of his average employees, while the cooperation's founding family owned US$90b equivalent to the wealth of the bottom 40 per cent of the US population' (Judt 2010, pp.5-6). Today, the richest one per cent in America owns more wealth than the bottom 90 per cent (Kristof 2014). The US therefore constitutes a divided society with an extremely wealthy top one per cent, and a very poor bottom ten per cent (Chetty et al. 2014).

Second, unequal access to education expands US income inequality. For example, in 2012, 42.4 per cent Americans aged 25-64 did not attain tertiary education; 7.1 per cent of youth aged 15-19 were neither employed nor in school; and 18.5 per cent of youth aged 20-24 were unemployed and not in school (OCED 2014a). Therefore 35.6 per cent Americans aged 15-24 were neither in school nor employed in 2012. Additionally, children from underprivileged districts drop out of school compared to those from mid-range income parents in wealthier states. 'Poor kids who remain in school perform poorly and obtain less fulfilling and lower-paid employment' (Judt 2010, pp.6). Combined education and racial factors project even more striking disparity. For instance, in 2008 the life expectancies of white American women and men with 16 years or more of schooling were far greater than black Americans with 'fewer than 12 years of education'

(Olshansky et al. 2012, p.1). Furthermore, US educational system is one of the most unequal because students receive different learning opportunities based on social status (Darling-Hammond & Post 2000). Children born into poor families fail to enter college. The demand for university students is 'kept artificially low based on institutional rules, rather than price signals' (Grusky & Weeden 2014, p.483). Due to the institutionalized bottlenecks, the supply of college-educated labour stagnates in a period of rising returns (Goldin & Katz, 2008). Only '30 per cent of each birth cohort now earns a college degree, just a little more than in the 1970s' (Hout 2009 & 2012 cited in Grusky & Weeden 2014, p.482). Today, about 8 per cent of Americans in the bottom half get a college education (Stiglitz 2014).

Last, unequal access to health leads to high inequality in America (Olshansky et al. 2012). Empirical studies posit that from 1980 to 2000, 'the life expectancy of the bottom ten per cent increased at only half the rate of the top ten, thus translating into an increase in health welfare' (Becker & Gordon 2008). Residents of wealthy districts live longer than those from poorer ones. Girls from poorer states experience teenage pregnancy, and their children are less likely to survive compared to their colleagues in wealthier states (Judt 2010). These gaps have widened over time leading to at least two "Americas". Although America devotes 17 per cent of its GDP to health care compared with nine per cent in Britain, nearly 50m Americans were uninsured in 2012, and life expectancy is slightly below average for a rich country (The Economist 2014a).

4. EDUCATION A PATHWAY TO REDUCING US INCOME AND OPPORTUNITY INEQUALITY

Even though there are several reform options to address America's income and opportunity inequality, health reform is one of the key priorities that the government could undertake. Good health might increase working hours and enhance productivity, but it might not directly increase income and expand opportunities. Conversely, health takes up more government transfers. For instance, in 2012, the US Government health spending was 50 per cent higher than in Britain. Employer-sponsored coverage is tax exempt, costing the government at least US$200b annually (The

Economist 2014a). These subsidies drive health-care inflation and favour rich employees. US private health care system is 'arguably inefficient, spending twice the health percentage of Australia's GDP, but producing poorer results exemplified by a shorter life expectancy of three years' compared to Australia (Stiglitz 2014, p.1).

Consequently, investment in equal access to quality education constitutes the most effective long-term reform to address the growing inequality in America and expand opportunities for all (OECD 2014b). According to the US Secretary of Education, Arne Duncan, 'the performance of American students in the latest PISA evaluation reflected a picture of educational stagnation' (OECD 2014b, p.13). There is also a declining trend to higher educational attainment and better skills. Empirical evidence shows that education and income are positively correlated in the US. For example, 'only college graduates have experienced uninterrupted growth in median weekly earnings from 1979 to 2009, while high school dropouts have seen a decline in theirs by about 22 per cent' (Hipple 2009).

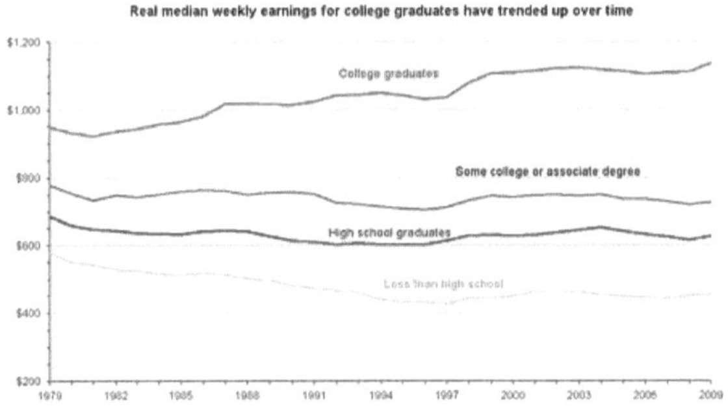

Source: US Bureau of Labor Statistics, 2009

To improve equal access to quality education, the government must take series of actions. First, it must invest in education at the early childhood period and enforce compulsory education (OECD 2014b). Second, the recommendations in the 'Race to the Top (RTT) program launched in 2010' (p.13), which amongst other things encourage states to transform lowest-performing schools and improve their programs of early learning and care (Denk et al., 2013), need to be funded and implemented. Third, the government must increase transfers for tertiary and college education and raise skills development spending for non-school going citizens dependent on the dynamic labour markets. This will ensure equality of opportunity for disadvantaged children, and link new graduates as well as re-trained professionals with jobs.

Last, the relatively low wages of teachers need to be increased. American high-school teachers with 15 years of experience get about 65 per cent of the income of a tertiary-educated individual working in other professions, compared to 85 per cent OECD average (OECD 2011). Low teaching wages lead to the least-qualified teachers teaching the least advantaged students. Perhaps, quality of teacher differences represents the fundamental school resource differential between minority and white children, and that explains much of the variance in student socioeconomic achievements (Darling-Hammond & Post 2000). In fact, disparate educational outcomes for the poor and minority children are 'much more a function of their unequal access to key educational resources, including skilled teachers and quality curriculum, compared to race or class' (p.128).

There are key challenges to this policy reform. First, it is a long term one, and inadequate resources might hamper its implementation. However, evidence shows that 'fiscal policy reduces income inequality' (Bastagli et al. 2012, p.3), and '54 per cent Americans support taxing the rich to aid the poor' (PRC 2014, p.1). Therefore, government must increase progressive income taxes on the wealthy (AEI 2014; Tanzi 2011) as a short-term strategy to increase national savings and expand social spending on the poor. More savings will provide resources to support the education reform budget. Progressive taxes should be complemented by taxes on capital gains from bequeathed and inherited assets (OECD 2014b, p.14). The government must improve tax compliance, abolish tax deductions disproportionately beneficial to the rich, and cut unnecessary overseas military spending to fund the education sector which has witnessed budget cuts (Kristof 2011). Second, policy divergence between Democrats and Republicans might block this reform. However, Democrats constitute the majority in the Senate and House of Representatives; thus, these policy reforms will successfully pass through Congress.

REFERENCES

American Enterprises Institute (AEI) for Public Policy Research 2014, *Political Report: a monthly poll compilation*, vol. 10, issue 2, AEI, viewed 26 September 2014, <*http://www.aei.org/files/2014/02/03/-aei-political-report-february-2014_154750338937.pdf*>.

Bastagli, F, Coady, D & Gupta S 2012, *Income inequality and fiscal policy*, IMF Staff Discussion Note 12/08, Washington DC, USA.

Chetty, R, Hendren, N, Kline, P, Saez, E & Turner, N 2014, 'Is the United States still a land of opportunity? recent trends in intergenerational mobility', NBER Working Paper No. 19844, viewed 21 September 2014; <http://www.equality-of-opportunity.org/files/mobility_trends.pdf>.

Darling-Hammond, L & Post, L 2000, 'Inequality in teaching and schooling: supporting high-quality teaching and leadership in low-income-schools', in Richard D. Kahlenberg, (ed), *A Nation at Risk: Preserving Public Education as an Engine for Social Mobility*, The Century Foundation, USA.

Denk, O, Hagemann, R, Lenain, P & Somma V 2013, 'Inequality and poverty in the United States: public policies for inclusive growth', OECD Working Paper 1052, Paris, view 18 September 2014, <http://www.oecd.org/officialdocuments/publicdisplaydocument pdf/?cote=ECO/WKP(2013)44&docLanguage=En>.

Dew-Becker, I, Gordon, R 2008, 'Controversies about the Rise of American Inequality: A Survey', National Bureau of Economic Research (NBER) Working Paper Series, no. 1050, Massachusetts Avenue, Cambridge, MA 02138, viewed 15 September 2014, <http://www.nber.org/papers/w13982>.

Goda, T 2013, 'Changes in the income inequality from a global perspective: an overview, Post Keynesian Economics Study Group', Working Paper, no. 1303, Mdellin, Colombia.

Goldin, C, & Katz, L 2008, *The race between education and technology*, Harvard University Press, Cambridge, MA.

Grusky, D & Weeden, K 2014, 'Inequality and market failure 2014', *American Behavioral Scientist*, vol.57, pp. 3-7 (online), viewed 18 September 2014,
<http://abs.sagepub.com/content/58/3/473>.

Hipple, S 2009, Bureau of Labor Statistics, *Charting the U.S. Labor Market in 2006 updated 2009*; viewed 21 September 2014,
<http://economix.blogs.nytimes.com/2010/05/17/the-value-of-college-2/>.

Judt, T 2010, *Ill fares the land*, New York Review of Books, New York, USA.

Kristof, N 2014, 'An idiot's guide to inequality', *New York Times* (online), 23 July, viewed 26 September 2014,
<http://www.nytimes.com/2014/07/24/opinion/nicholas-kristof-idiots-guide-to-inequality-piketty-capital.html?_r=0>.
______ 2011, 'Our broken escalator', *New York Times* (online), 16 July, viewed 26 September 2014,
<http://www.nytimes.com/2011/07/17/opinion/sunday/17kristof.html?_r=0>.

Organization for Economic Cooperation and Development (OECD) 2008, *Growing unequal? Income distribution and poverty in OECD countries*, OECD, Paris, France.
<http://www.oecd.org/els/soc/41527936.pdf>.

______2011, *Education at a glance, OECD indicators*, OECD, viewed 20 September 2014,
<http://www.oecd.org/education/skills-beyond-school/48631582.pdf>.

______2014a, *Country statistical profile: United States, Country statistical profiles: Key tables from OECD*, viewed 20 September 2014
<http://www.oecd-ilibrary.org/economics/country-statistical-profile-united-states_20752288-table-usa>.

______2014b, *United States tackling high inequalities creating opportunities for all June 2014, OECD*, viewed 20 September 2014, <http://www.oecd.org/unitedstates/Tackling-high-inequalities.pdf>.

Olshansky, J, et al., (2012), 'Differences in life expectancy due to race and educational differences are widening, and many may not catch up', *Health Affairs*, vol. 31, no. 8, pp.1803-1813.

PEW Research Centre (PRC) 2014, *Most See Inequality Growing, but Partisans Differ over Solutions, 23 January 2014*, PEW, viewed 18 September 2014, <file:///C:/Users/Helen.garbo/Desktop/ANU%202nd%20Sem%202014/Crawford%208000/Readings/US%20Inequality/PEW%201-23-14%20Poverty_Inequality%20Release.pdf>.

Stiglitz, J 2014, 'Inequality: why Australia must not follow the US', *The Sydney Morning Herald* (online), 6 July, viewed 10 September 2014 <http://www.smh.com.au/comment/inequality-why-australia-must-not-follow-the-us-20140706-zsxtk.html>.

Tanzi, V 2011, 'Equity, transparency, cooperation and the taxation of high net worth individuals', Paper Presented at the Fourth International Tax Dialogue on 'Tax and Equity' 7-9 December, New Delhi, India.

The Economist 2014a, 'Health care in America, how to fix Obamacare: America's health-care system remains dysfunctional, but it could be made better', *The Economist* (online), 20 September, viewed 21 September 2014, <http://www.economist.com/news/leaders/21618788-americas-health-care-system-remains-dysfunctional-it-could-be-made-better-how-fix>.

The Economist 2014b, 'Inequality and the narrowing tax base: Too reliant on the few-Taxes are best raised on a broad base, but in many countries, it is worryingly narrow', *The Economist* (online), 20 September, viewed 21 September 2014, <http://www.economist.com/news/leaders/21618784-taxes-are-best-raised-broad-base-many-countries-it-worryingly-narrow-too-reliant>.

The World Bank 2008, Commission on Growth and Development (CGD) 2008, *The policy ingredients of growth strategies; Part 2, the growth report: strategies for sustained growth and inclusive development*, World Bank, Washington DC.

INDONESIA AND THE PROBLEM OF TRANSBOUNDARY HAZE POLLUTION

1. INTRODUCTION

Transboundary haze pollution (THP) is one of Southeast Asia's intractable environmental problems (Forsyth 2014). It originates from Indonesia and spreads to neighboring countries (Bell 2 014). THP results from 'fire outbreaks leading to suspended thick smoke in the atmosphere pushed by air from Indonesia into Singapore, Malaysia, Thailand and other neighboring states' (Florano 2004, p.2). Haze pollution occurs during dry seasons when forest and peat swamps are more flammable. In 1997, THP became a prominent regional problem (Forsyth 2014, p.5), and hit its highest air pollution record in 2005 and 2013 (p.3). The Indonesian National Disaster and Mitigation Agency has announced that the suppression of current fires, 66 per cent of which started in oil palm, logging and pulpwood concessions, will cost Rp 355b or US\$ 30m (Bell 2014). THP has huge environmental, economic and health consequences, and has so far withstood both national and regional solutions, hence it is a "wicked problem". This essay argues that Singapore should institute a pollution reduction certification regime for all forest and agricultural imports from Indonesia. This might pressure investment companies and Indonesia to reduce haze pollution.

2. KEY ISSUE IN THE CASE

Haze consists of enough smoke, dust, moisture, and vapor suspended in the air thus impairing visibility (ASEAN 2014a). It becomes "transboundary" if its density and extent is so great and remains at measurable levels after crossing into another country's air space (ASEAN 2014a). THP risks biodiversity, releases greenhouse gases, undermines tourism and economic activities, and threatens diplomatic relations in Southeast Asia (Forsyth 2014, p5). The 1997 THP was considered one of the biggest environmental shocks in history (UNEP 1999). It destroyed a combined 9.9m hectares of Indonesian agricultural land, peat swamp and forest (BAPPENAS 1999). Also, 236 passengers and crew died on 26 September 1997 in an Air Garuda plane crash due to poor visibility, and 29 passengers and crew got killed when a ship collided with a supertanker on said day (CRWF 800 Case Pack 2013, pp. 108-109).

Furthermore, over 70m people were regionally affected, while 40,000 were hospitalized and treated for smog related sicknesses (Florano 2004). The region lost about US$1.4b with Malaysia and Singapore losing US$310m and US$74m respectively (EEPSAA/WWF 2003). Approximately 100,000 square kilometers of Indonesia's forests and peat swamps got burnt costing the country US$9b in terms of economic, social and environmental losses, and about 1 to 2 billion tons of carbon were emitted (Bell 2014, ASEAN 2014b). Singapore witnessed its 'highest Pollutant Standards Index (PSI) in 2013 with an unprecedented level of 401' (Forsyth 2014, p.5). It therefore strongly supports haze pollution reduction.

3. THEORETICALLY INFORMED DISCUSSION OF THE ISSUE

Transboundary haze pollution has four main causes. First, it results from prolonged drought referred to as El Nino that facilitates large fire outbreaks (ASEAN 2014a). Second, indiscriminate logging activities in Indonesia's forests cause THP. For instance, loggers burn forests to gain access to valuable trees. Burning methods cost US$180 to access 1 hectare of timber plantation on peat soil compared to US$800 per hectare when non-burning methods are used (Tacconi et al. 2008). These logging activities include illegal logging that destroyed over 40 per cent of Indonesia's 160m hectares of forests (King 1996, p. 216), and led to loss of US$1b annually (Mongabay.com 2006). Third, local farmers and agricultural companies use burning as a more cost-effective means to cultivate the forest land for agricultural purposes. Last, peat fires produce significant amount of smoke containing concentrated carbon dioxide. In 2006, Indonesian peat land and fossil fuel combustion accounted for 40 per cent of global carbon dioxide emission (Silvius et al. 2006).

Singaporean and Malaysian companies closely linked to governments are mostly responsible for the deforestation and fires in Indonesia. They 'burn forests and peat with impunity due to strong connections with their governments and local politicians' (Varkkey 2013, p.381). Colfer (2005) indicates that 'companies can use fire to compete for land concessions, and as aggressive acts to destroy competing plantations or put them in a bad record' (p. 120). National and regional efforts to reduce haze pollution are hindered by rampant corruption, weak implementation capacity of anti-haze pollution laws, unclear property rights of concessions, illegal logging, and rent seeking among local Indonesian authorities (Schonhardt 2013). Generally, THP is a classic example of the challenge developing countries face in balancing economic growth and environmental sustainability.

There have been national, bilateral and regional efforts to resolve haze pollution problem. Nationally, Indonesia has instituted a selective cutting policy (Dauvergne 1993, p.7), restricted peat swamps as protected lands (Silvius & Suryadiputra 2005), legalized revocation of licenses of companies found burning forests, and the imprisonment of those causing forests and peat fires for ten years as well as payment of RP 10b as fine (Hon 2014)). These policies failed to curb haze pollution due to implementation failures and corruption in Indonesia (Maryudi 2009).

Singapore, Malaysia and Australian pursue bilateral engagements with Indonesia to address transboundary haze pollution. Between 2007 and 2011, Singapore implemented a US$1m joint project with the Indonesian Jambi Province to address haze pollution. The project, amongst others, trained local provincial officials to monitor fire sources, and to interpret satellite images (ASEAN 2007). Malaysia and Indonesia on the other hand signed a Memorandum of Understanding to address haze pollution in the Riau province (International Peat Society 2009). The project supported fire prevention and control awareness, the development of early warning systems, and the promotion of 'zero burning' methods amongst plantations and local farmers (Strait Times 2007). For its part, Australia invested AU$30m under the Forest Carbon Partnership programme in the Kalimantan province to help rehabilitate and protect over 100,000 hectares of peat land (REDD Desk 2014).

In addition to national and bilateral efforts, the Association of Southeast Asian Nations (ASEAN) founded in 1967 (Ravenhill 2009) adopted the 2002 THP Agreement, which constitutes the only regional treaty on THP committing parties to international cooperation and domestic actions to prevent fires (Nguitragool 2011). This treaty became effective in 2003 after all members states signed and ratified, except for Indonesia that ratified 12 years later in September 2014 (Bell 2014). However, given that international treaties tend to balance national interest against international interests, it is unclear whether Indonesia will implement its side of the bargain.

4.   TRADE BARRIER AS PATHWAY TO ADDRESS THP

Although THP in Southeast Asia defies national and regional solutions, Singapore is adopting national reforms to help address the problem. The country calls for public sharing of concession maps and official land use to indicate companies' concessions locations, but Indonesia and Malaysia disagree on legal grounds (Hon 2014). Singapore's parliament has therefore approved a bill to penalize both foreign and Singaporean investment companies involved in haze pollution in Indonesia (Shen 2014). This bill proposes fines up to US$80,000 for each day that companies contribute to air pollution through burning on their plantations (Butler 2014). International law permits extraterritorial jurisdiction provided the conduct affects the state asserting such jurisdiction; hence a government can prosecute culprits for activities conducted outside its territory (Ewing-Chow & Koh 2013). However, this is unlikely if such culprits cannot easily be identified.

Consequently, Singapore should institute a haze pollution reduction certification regime on all forest and agricultural products originating from Indonesia. The government should set up a national commission that will certificate qualified companies, and clear imports that meet the haze pollution standards agreed under the ASEAN treaty. This might pressure the Indonesian government and Singaporean investment companies in Indonesia to address haze pollution because they need the Singaporean market and Investment opportunities. In 2012 'Singapore was Indonesia's top foreign investor, with a cumulative total of US$1.14b in 142 investment projects' (Jakarta Globe 2012). The country is the biggest importer of wood products from Indonesia. Bilateral trade between the two countries reached US$79.4b in 2013, making Indonesia Singapore's third largest trading partner (Singapore Government 2014), a status Indonesia wishes to improve upon (Jakarta Globe 2012). This certification regime might therefore influence companies producing and exporting forest and agricultural products to Singapore to reduce haze pollution. Investment companies that would comply may get tax breaks as an incentive.

To regionalize this policy, Singapore should lobby other ASEAN member states to adopt the certification regime on a regional level to complement the ASEAN haze treaty. This might increase regional pressure on Indonesia to implement agreed haze pollution reduction policies. If other member states disapprove, Singapore should request the World Trade Organization to endorse the certification regime, thus internationalizing the haze pollution problem and bringing Indonesia under international environmental pollution spotlight. This might bring additional pressure to bear on Indonesia. Evidence shows that Indonesia fears being complained at the international level for haze pollution. For instance, in 2006, when Singapore elevated the issue of THP at the United Nations, Indonesia became uncomfortable and opted for a regional solution under ASEAN (Jakarta Post 2006 cited in CRWF 8000 Case Pack 2013). Singapore's action might therefore make Indonesia enforce bans on burning of peat and forests by investment companies and local farmers. Reduced burning will lower haze pollution. Furthermore, environmental interest groups in the ASEAN region might put additional pressure on Indonesia and investment companies from Malaysia and Singapore to reduce haze pollution. With such concerted pressure, Indonesia might take tougher actions against haze polluters.

Because trade barriers reduce exports and imports (Gans et al. 2012), this policy might reduce consumers' choices in Singapore, and impose a cost on the traded goods, thus raising local prices. The trade barriers might generally reduce economic efficiency and spark diplomatic tensions. However, not all imports from Indonesia are inclusive. Conversely, Singapore can import goods from other sources. After all, 'Indonesia has the technology and enforcement capacity to impose and enforce bans on burning of forests and peat land' (CIFOR 2013). Therefore, Singapore should adopt this national policy reform. The certification commission would be funded under the national budget of Singapore.

Aggarwal, V, Chow, J 2010, 'The perils of consensus: how ASEAN's meta-regime undermines economic and environmental cooperation', *Review of International Political Economy,* vol. 17, pp. 262-290.

ASEAN 2014a, Information on haze fires, Association of South East Asian Nations, viewed on 17 October 2014, <http://haze.asean.org/?page_id=249>.

ASEAN 2014b, Combating haze in ASEAN: frequently asked questions, Association of South East Asian Nations, viewed 17 October 2014, <http://haze.asean.org/?page_id=113#1>.

ASEAN 2007, ASEAN document series 2007, Association of Southeast Asia Nations, viewed 20 October 2014, <http://www.asean.org/archive/5187-12.pdf>.

ASEAN 2002, *ASEAN Agreement on Transboundary Haze Pollution,* Association of South East Asian Nations Secretariat, Jakarta.

Asia-Pacific Economic Cooperation (APEC) 2014, *ASEAN 2007 Ministerial Meetings on Transboundary Haze Pollution*, APEC, viewed 16 October 2014, <egs.apec.org/more-articles/159-asean-ministerial-meetings-on-transboundary-haze-pollution>.

BAPPENAS 1999, *Causes, extent, impact and costs of 1997/1998 fires and drought: final report*, Annex 1 and 2, Planning for Fire Prevention and Drought Management Project, National Development Planning Agency (BAPPENAS), and Asian Development Bank (ADB), Jakarta.

Bell, L 2014, 'After 12 years, Indonesia finally ratifies transboundary haze agreement', Mongabay.com (online edition), 18 September, viewed 15 October 2014,

REFERENCES

<http://news.mongabay.com/2014/0920-lbell-indonesia-haze-transboundary-agreement.html>.

Bhattacharya, J, Pye, O 2013, 'The palm oil controversy in Southeast Asia: a transnational perspective', Institute of Southeast Asian Studies, Singapore.

Butler, R 2014, 'Singapore to fine domestic, foreign companies for causing haze', Mongabay.com (online edition), 7 August, viewed 15 October 2014, <http://news.mongabay.com/2014/0806-singapore-transboundary-haze-pollution-bill.html>.

Center for International Forestry Research (CIFOR) 2013, Q&A on first and haze in Southeast Asia, CIFOR, viewed 14 October 2014, <http://blog.cifor.org/17591/qa-on-fires-and-haze-in-southeast-asia#.VEIL2PnF94->.

Colfer, C.J.P 2000, 'Causes and impacts of forest fires: a case study from East Kalimantan,
Indonesia', International Forest Fire News vol. 22, pp. 35-40.

Colfer, C.J.P 2005, 'The complex forest: communities, uncertainty, and adaptive
collaborative management', Resources for the Future, Washington DC.

Cotton, J 1999, 'The "haze" over Southeast Asia: challenging the ASEAN mode of regional engagement', *Pacific Affairs*, vol. 72, pp. 331-351.

Crawford 8000 2014, CRWF 8000 Case Pack 2013, Crawford School of Economics and Government, Australian National University, pp. 108-109.

Dauvergne, P 1993, 'The Politics of Deforestation in Indonesia', *Pacific Affairs*, vol 66, no. 4, pp. 497-518.

Ewing-Chow, M, Koh, T 2013, 'The transboundary haze and the international law', The Jakarta Post (Oneline edition) 27 June 2013), viewed 19 October 2-14,

<http://lkyspp.nus.edu.sg/ips/wp-content/uploads/sites/2/2013/07/pa_TK_Jakarta-Post_The-transboundary-haze-and-the-international-law_270613.pdf>.

EEPSEA/WWF 2003, The Indonesian fires and haze of 1997: The economic toll", Economy and Environment Program for Southeast Asia (EEPSEA) and Worldwide Fund for Nature (WWF).

Florano, E. R, 2004, 'The case of the ASEAN Regional Haze Action Plan', International Environmental Governance Conference, Paris 15 & 16 March 2004, viewed October 2014,
<http://www.cleanairinitiative.org/portal/sites/default/files/articles-69345_paper.pdf>.

Forsyth, T, 2014, 'Public concerns about transboundary haze: a comparison of Indonesia,
Singapore, and Malaysia', *Global Environmental Change*, vol. 25, pp.76-86.

Gans, J, King, S, Stonecash, R & Mankiw, G 2013, *Principles of Economics*, China Translation and Printing Services, Beijing, China.

Hon, R 2013, 'ASEAN: in a daze over the haze?' *The Singapore Law Review* (online edition), 25 December, viewed 14 October 2014,
<http://www.singaporelawreview.org/2013/12/asean-in-a-daze-over-the-haze/>.

International Peat Society (2009) "Malaysia and Indonesia Cooperate in Haze Fight". *Peat News*, 7/2009.

Jakarta Globe 2012, 'Yudhoyono wants more Singapore investors', Jakarta Globe (online edition), 22 July, viewed 22 October 2014,
<http://thejakartaglobe.beritasatu.com/archive/yudhoyono-wants-more-singapore-investors/454596/#Scene_1>.

King, D. Y, 1996, 'The Political Economy of Forest Sector Reform in Indonesia', *Journal of Environment and Development*, vol. 5, no. 2, pp. 216-232.

Nguitragool, P 2011, 'Negotiating the haze treaty: rationality and institutions in the
negotiations for the ASEAN Agreement on Transboundary Haze Pollution (2002)', *Asian
Survey*, vol. 51, pp. 356-378.

Ravenhill J 2009, 'East Asian regionalism: much ado about nothing?' *Review of International Studies*, vol. 35, pp. 215-235.

REED Desk 2014, Indonesia Australia forest carbon partnership, viewed 15 October 2014
<http://theredddesk.org/countries/initiatives/indonesia-australia-forest-carbon-partnership>.

Schonhardt, S 2013, 'How corruption is fuelling the haze', The Straits Times (online edition), 25 June, viewed 15 October 2014,
<http://www.straitstimes.com/the-big-story/asia-report/opinion/story/how-corruption-fuelling-the-haze-20130625>.

Shen, R 2014, 'Singapore approves bill to fine domestic, overseas air polluters', Reuters (online edition), 5 August, viewed 17 October 2014,
<http://www.reuters.com/article/2014/08/05/us-singapore-haze-lawmaking-idUSKBN0G50WB20140805>.

Silvius, M, Kaat, A, Van de Bund, H, Hooijer, A 2006, 'Peatland degradation fuels climate change', Wageningen, *Wetlands International*.

Silvius, M, Suryadiputra, N 2005, 'Review of policies and practices in tropical peat swamp forest management in Indonesia', *Wetlands International*.

Singapore Government 2014, Driving Singapore's external economy, Government of Singapore, viewed 22 October 2014,
<www.iesingapore.gov.sg/Venture-Overseas/Browse-By-Market/Asia-Pacific/Indonesia/Country-Information>.

Tacconi, L, Jotzo, F, Grafton, Q 2008, 'Local causes, regional co-operation and global financing for environmental problems: the case of Southeast Asian Haze pollution: International Environmental Agreements, *Politics, Law and Economics*, vol. 8, no. 1, pp. 1-16.

UNEP 1999, *Wildland fires and the environment: a global synthesis*, United Nations Environment Programme, Nairobi, viewed 18 October 2014, <http://www.fire.uni-freiburg.de/programmes/un/global-fire-UNEP.pdf>.

Varkkey, H 2013, 'Malaysian investors in the Indonesia oil palm plantation sector: home state facilitation and transboundary haze', *Asia Pacific Business Review*, vol.19, no.3, pp. 381-401.

PART V

INTERNATIONAL COOPERATION

WHAT WILL THE AFRICA-CHINA BILATERAL RELATIONSHIP LOOK LIKE IN 2030?

I. INTRODUCTION

This policy memo is directed to the Liberian Government. It considers potential changes in the level of trade between the People's Republic of China (PRC) and Africa over a 15-year period and advises the Liberian Government how to respond in the event each of the scenarios discussed comes to pass. This memo is about trade cooperation. It focuses on scenarios for Africa's future, which might have implications for the level of trade between Africa and its largest trading partner, China (Xinhua 2013), and could therefore impact on Liberia.

CURRENT SITUATION

Africa and China are strategic partners through the Forum on China-Africa Cooperation (FOCAC) established in 2000 to promote political dialogue and trade between the two sides (Africa's Strategic Partnerships 2009, p. 3). China has become Africa's largest trade partner, and Africa is presently China's major import source, second largest overseas construction project contract market, and fourth largest investment destination (Xinhua 2013). In 2005, China cancelled USD1.27b debt for 31 African states (Tull

2006), and declared the China-Africa Policy, underpinned by mutual respect for sovereignty, equitable economic cooperation and cultural exchange (China-African Policy 2006).

China holds a greater share of power and influence in this relationship due to its unconditional aid, grants, concessional loans, and increasing foreign direct investment in Africa. For instance, Chinese FDI in Africa reached USD16b in 2011(Enuka 2011). China has also increased its financial assistance to the region, including the provision of a credit facility of USD20b through the FOCAC framework (FOCAC 2012). In 2012, China constructed the USD200m 20 story Office Complex in Addis Ababa, Ethiopia 'as a gift to the African Union (AU)' (China-Africa Economic Trade Cooperation 2013, p.14). Africa is China's main natural resource and raw materials import source. China imports oil and gas, minerals, farm products and timber from Africa, while Africa imports machinery, equipment, vehicles, consumer electronics, textiles and clothing from China (Chaponniere 2009). Africa-China trade is strong, reaching USD198.49b in 2012, and USD210.2b in 2013 with exports to Africa at USD92.8b, up 8.8 per cent, while imports from Africa hit USD117.4b, up 3.8 per cent (Xinhua Global Times 2014). Most African states support the 'One China Policy'.

On 5 May 2014, Premier Li Keqiang officially visited Africa. During this visit, China and Africa, through the African Union Commission (AUC), agreed to implement the outcomes of President Xi's 2013 Africa visit, and to further strengthen Africa-China cooperation (PRC MFA 2014). Premier Li also attended the Plenary Session of the 24th World Economic Forum on Africa in Abuja, Nigeria on 8 May 2014.

Two key drivers might affect Africa-China trade in the next 15 years.

II. DRIVERS

DRIVER ONE: POLITICAL INSTABILITY: CONFLICT AND INSECURITY VS. PEACE AND STABILITY

Political instability and terrorism threaten peace and security in Africa. Insecurity is therefore important to Africa-China trade because it might increase fragility in the region and undermine the level of trade between

Africa and China in the next 15 years. For example, political instability in the Central African Republic and the natural resource rich Democratic Republic of Congo undermines peace, stability and trade between those conflict states and other states including China. These conflicts might escalate in the next 15 years, thereby destabilizing the Central African region (UNSG Briefing 2014). Also, piracy attacks in the Gulf of Guinea, which sharply increased in number and intensity in 2012, might worsen and impose greater security spending on governments in that region, push shipment costs higher, and disrupt trade on the continent (Global Economic Prospects 2014). Additionally, the increasing instability and terrorism in Nigeria, Africa's largest economy (Aljazeera 2014), is an 'important security problem that might negatively affect trade and economic activities in the subregion' (Africa's Economic Outlook 2014, p. 88).

In South Africa, the continent's second largest economy, structural bottlenecks and tense labour relations combined with weak external demand kept growth slower at 1.9 per cent and could be further exacerbated to retard growth in the next 15 years (Global Economic Prospects 2014). Lastly, persistent political instability in several African states including Egypt, Libya, South Sudan, Sudan, Somalia, Ethiopia, Cote d'Ivoire, and sporadic terrorist attacks in Mali and Kenya (BBC African News 2014) are significant security risks that might deteriorate to undermine Africa-China trade in the next decades. For instance, the conflict in South Sudan presently has displaced 1.8m persons, thereby increasing humanitarian need in that region. The United Nations presently needs USD1.8b to deal with this humanitarian crisis (ABC News 2014). Conflict and instability in Africa will therefore disrupt peace and stability, retard economic growth and development, increase famine, heighten humanitarian crisis, further impoverish the population, and ultimately weaken Africa-China trade by 2030.

Conversely, some optimists argue that Africa is on an irreversible path to peace and stability. They maintain that most African states are democratic, pointing out that this might enhance peace and stability, and spur regional growth and development in the coming decades (UNECA & AU Economic Report on Africa 2013). These optimists maintain that the new generation of African leaders, through the AU, have adopted strategic measures to enhance democratic governance. For instance, the

New Economic Partnership for Africa's Development (NEPAD) was formed to foster democratic governance (AU Report 2014). NEPAD, they contend will enhance democracy, human rights and peace in Africa (Bratton & van de Walle 1998). NEPAD has in return yielded an African Peer Review Mechanism (APRM), enabling African states to review and track each other's democratic achievements and failures annually, and this might consolidate democratic governance in the next 15 years (NEPAD Report 2013).

Additionally, the AU has constituted an African Standby Force (ASF), which in a decade might be capacitated to intervene in member states to forestall civil unrests (AU 2013). This would allow the AU to intervene in conflicts without usual delays resulting from dependence on the UN. Furthermore, the African Court for Human and People's Rights (ACHPR) might become vibrant, serving as a hedge against human rights abuses and crimes against humanity in Africa by 2030, thus curbing conflicts, and enhancing peace, justice and stability. Peace and security will create a democratic space, and an enabling environment for investment, ultimately leading to economic growth and development (AU PSC 2014). Political stability will therefore result in stronger trade between Africa and China in 15 years.

DRIVER TWO: ECONOMIC GROWTH: ECONOMIC GROWTH VS. ECONOMIC DECLINE

Economic growth is another key driver that will impact Africa-China trade in 15 years. Growth is extremely important because the level of trade with Africa depends on how the economy in the region improves, stagnates or declines. Africa's real GDP is expected to grow at 5.3 per cent in 2014, 5.7 per cent in 2015 and 6.5 per cent in 2016 (IMF 2014; UN 2014). Hence, as peace and stability thrive, trade in oil, gas, mining and non-extractive industry might significantly increase, doubling Africa's growth rate at 12 per cent in 2030. Africa-China trade, currently USD210b, might concurrently double, reaching USD420b in 15 years. FDI may simultaneously expand. Net FDI flows, which rose from USD37b in 2012 to USD43b, growing at 16 percent in 2013 (The World Bank 2014), might consistently increase by six billion annually, reaching USD133b in 2030.

Furthermore, tourism, an important driver of growth in Sub-Saharan Africa, continues to grow at a robust pace. The UN World Tourism Organization (UNWTO) data shows that tourist arrivals in the region grew by 6.0 percent in 2013, higher than the annual growth of 4.4 percent in 2012 (UNECA & AU Africa Economic Report 2014). International tourist arrivals in the region are expected to double in next few years, and triple in a decade and half reaching 18 per cent by 2030. This will confirm UNWTO estimated tourist expansion, adding to the region's economic growth. Also, infrastructure development on the continent might boost agricultural productivity, raising Africa's per capita GDP over the medium term (AfDB 2012). In 2012 the continent's per capita GDP grew at around 3 per cent and might also double in a decade and half reaching 6 per cent in 2025. Ongoing infrastructural projects in Africa might link growth corridors, enhance intra Africa trade, increase domestic consumption and attract high foreign direct and foreign portfolio investments (World Bank 2013; AfDB 2012). This may also upsurge agricultural output and productivity, and promote tourism, thereby enhancing economic growth in Africa. The impressive economic prospect, underpinned by increasing double digit growth rate, and growing investment due to peace and stability might lead to stronger Africa-China trade by 2030.

Conversely, economic growth might decline dropping from 6.0 per cent to 3.0 per cent. This might result from several factors. First, a 2013 baseline study suggests that the price of oil which boosted growth in the region will decline by about 1.3 percentage points and current account balances will deteriorate by 4.5 percentage (Africa's Economic Outlook 2014). Also, the expected boom in the US oil and gas supplies could eclipse supplies from Africa and Asia by 2020 (Blackwill & O'Sullivan 2014). This may inhibit Africa's growth, which is largely dependent on oil and gas exports. Second, poor physical infrastructure, including unreliable electricity supplies and poor transport systems, might impede economic growth and development. Third, instability and terrorism in Africa might exacerbate, thereby destroying existing infrastructure and preventing investment in new infrastructure on the continent (AICD Report 2010). Fourth, expected droughts will pose a threat to agricultural productivity and increase famine as most countries in the region depend on rain-fed subsistence agriculture for their economies and livelihoods

(UNECA Report 2014). The resulting lower local harvests might raise the risk of food insecurity and push food prices higher, dampening household consumption, which has been another important driver of growth in the region in recent years. Last, Africa has not translated its growth story into economic diversification and social development. Therefore, economic activities depend heavily on exports of raw materials, with too little value addition, and few forward and backward linkages to other sectors of the economy. All these factors combined might hamper economic growth and weaken Africa-China trade by 2030.

Combining the effects of these two drivers, four plausible scenarios can be produced to examine how Africa-China trade might unfold in 15 years. Two of the four scenarios are outlined in detail.

Peace and Security in Africa

Africa rising, China falters   **Africa: the growth angel**

Economic Stagnation ← → Economic
in China   Growth in China

Africa: the failing promise   **China rising, Africa falters**

Civil unrest and instability in Africa

III. SCENARIOS

SCENARIO ONE: AFRICA THE GROWTH ANGEL

In 2030, Africa is peaceful, stable and safe for trade and investment. Predictions that Nigeria, the continent's largest economy (Aljazeera 2014), would erupt into full scale civil war, thereby adversely affecting trade and economic activities in the subregion (Africa's Economic Outlook 2014, p. 88), have failed. The country's GDP of USD510b has doubled in 15 years reaching USD1.2 trillion. In South Africa, the continent's second largest economy, growth rises doubling the 2013 GDP of USD390b to USD780b. This leap is caused by improved labour standards in mining areas, leading to increased productivity and output. Peace and stability in the Central African region thrive, contradicting predictions that the conflicts in the Central African Republic and the Democratic Republic of Congo would undermine regional peace, stability and trade (UNSG Briefing 2014). At long last, peace and stability prevail in the Democratic Republic of Congo, Central African Republic, et al. thus leading to mining boom in the mineral resource rich central African region. Global energy security concerns have led African states, China, the US and the EU to contain piracy in the Gulf of Guinea, reducing shipment cost and creating safer trade routes, disproving 2014 claims that piracy would escalate and impose greater security spending on governments, push shipment costs higher, and disrupt international trade (Global Economic Prospects 2014). National security spending on piracy reduces; government's shifts spending to improved infrastructure and economic empowerment programmes. Peace and stability in Egypt, Libya, South Sudan, Sudan, Somalia, Mali, Kenya, Cote d'Ivoire and other African states reign, as civil unrests and terrorist attacks disappear.

Amidst thriving peace, democratic governance takes root as most African states hold democratic elections and deepen respect for human rights and dignity, thereby enhancing peace and stability and development. Increased stability attracts increased investment, leading to stronger trade, growth and development (UNECA & AU Economic Report on Africa 2013). The New Economic Partnership for Africa's Development becomes a vibrant Pan-African democratic and governance institute, also consolidating good governance, human rights and peace (Bratton & van de Walle 1998) on the continent. The African Peer-review Mechanism (APRM) is robust as the remaining 32 African states accede to the APRM. All states peer-reviewed by 2030, thereby increasing governance, accountability and transparency on the continent. The African Stand by Force (ASF) is fully functional, equipped with the necessary logistics, manpower, and fully funded to intervene in member states to forestall civil unrests (AU Peace and Security Council 2013). Simultaneously, all African states accede to the Africa Charter on Human and People's Rights

(ACHPR). The African Court for Human and People's Rights (ACHPR) is fully functional, serving as a hedge against human rights abuses and crimes against humanity in Africa (ACHPR 2013). Human rights abusers, terrorists and troublemakers arrested, prosecuted and punished by the ACHPR. Peace and security are consolidated, allowing full implementation of the AU regional integration strategic plan (AU Strategic Plan 2013). Intra Africa trade rises, as integration advances due to improved infrastructure, providing an enabling environment for investment, economic growth and development (AU PSC 2014).

A stable international and regional order has advanced an atmosphere under which Africa's economy has prospered. Under said global environment, China's economy thrives, maintaining the predicted stable annual growth rate of 10 per cent (Subramanian 2011). The Global Trends 2030 fusion scenarios has played out (National Intelligence Council 2012), promoting US-China collaboration in pursuit of enhanced interdependence (Lind 2008). Strategic international cooperation deepens amidst a prosperous global economy. Africa's integration and intra continental trade are consolidated through stronger AU mechanisms. China remains the biggest trading partner of the region under a more liberalized communist party pursuing internal democratic reforms and a more open market economy. Africa-China trade grows stronger in this globally prosperous environment, reaching its all-time height, rising from USD210.2b (Xinhua Global Times 2014) to USD420.4b in 2030 with exports to Africa at USD183.6, while imports from Africa hit USD234.8b. Africa becomes the world's growth angel.

SCENARIO 2: AFRICA- THE FAILING PROMISE

By 2030, economic growth declines from its 2016 rate of 6.5 per cent (IMF 2014) to 3.0 per cent. The decline is prompted by several factors. First, the price of oil declines by about 1.3 percentage points and current account balances deteriorate by 4.5 percentage (Africa's Economic Outlook 2014). Concurrently, the expected boom in the US oil and gas supplies arrives, eclipsing supplies from Africa and Asia (Blackwill & O'Sullivan 2014). This dampens Africa's share of trade in oil and gas and inhibits Africa's growth, which is largely dependent on oil and gas exports (Global Economic Prospects 2014). Additionally, poor physical infrastructure, including unreliable electricity supply and poor transport system, remain widespread, impeding economic growth and development. Poor infrastructure undermines intra continental trade and agricultural productivity, subtracting their share from economic growth (AICD Report 2010). The continent's per capita GDP falls from 3 per cent to 1.5 per cent, declining from its 2012 growth rate (AfDB 2012).

The projected droughts arrive in 2030, intensifying famine mainly in the Horn of Africa, and posing a threat to agricultural output, dependent on rain-fed subsistence agriculture in most African countries. Inadequate rainfalls affect growth prospects in many African countries as was forecast by UN Economic Commission for African and the African Union (UNECA & AU Report 2014). The resulting lower local harvest increases food insecurity and pushes food prices higher. Households' consumption diminishes, thereby undermining another important driver of growth in the region. Africa-China trade currently USD210b equally declines by half, and net FDI flows, which rose from 37b USD in 2012 to USD43b, growing at 16 percent in 2013 (The World Bank 2014) fall back to USD37b in 2030. High inflation rates, massive unemployment, corruption and capital flight are entrenching Africa's macroeconomic misfortunes.

The economic stagnation is occasioned by political unrest, instability, and terrorism, thereby stalling investment in Africa. Nationalist scramble for power and control of, oil, gas, mining and other natural resources, increases fragility and undermines trade in the region. Political instability in the CAR and the DRC intensify with spill overs in neighbouring Republics of Congo, Gabon, Burundi, and Rwanda, further destabilizing the Central African region, affirming UNSG 2014 predictions (UNSG Briefing 2014). Piracy, in the Gulf of Guinea intensifies, imposes greater security spending on governments, pushes shipment costs higher, and disrupts trade on the continent (Global Economic Prospects 2014). Nigeria, Africa's largest economy (Aljazeera 2014), plunges into a full-scale civil war with separatists Boko Haram and the predominantly Muslim North fighting for independence. The country's GDP drops by half of its 2014 level, shrinking to USD255b. Nigeria's civil war exacerbates humanitarian crisis as millions of refugees spill over to neighbouring countries, disrupting trade and economic activities in the subregion (Africa's Economic Outlook 2014).

In contrast to the UNWTO prediction of growth in tourism by 6 per cent (Africa's Economic Report 2014), international tourist arrivals in the region wane to 3 per cent. Trafficking of small arms, adoptions, kidnapping, terrorist attacks and gun running increase in West Africa. Post conflict and fragile states including Sierra Leone, Liberia, Guinea, Cote d'Ivoire, Mali, Guinea Bissau, et al. are on the verge of relapsing into conflicts. In South Africa, the continent's second largest economy, intensified structural bottlenecks and violent labour strikes combined with weak external demand stagnate growth at its 2014 rate of 1.9 per cent. Persistent civil conflicts in Egypt, Libya, South Sudan, Sudan, Somalia, and terrorist attacks in Mali and Kenya (BBC African News 2014) have exploded to unimaginable levels. In 2030, these conflicts further disrupt peace and stability, lead to severe humanitarian crises, impoverish the population, and weaken Africa-China trade.

Africa's economic malady is unfolding in an uncertain global and regional climate. A world order similar to the Global Trends' 'Gini Out-of-the-Bottle' scenario (National Intelligence Council 2012) has played out. Although Lind (2011) argues that economic integration would prevent interstate conflicts in South East Asia, intrastate civil conflicts break out during the long-awaited democratic transitions in China and North Korea. Separatists from Xinjiang, home to the Turkic-speaking Muslim ethnic Uighur minority liable for terrorist attacks, including the Kunming train massacre (Wen 2014), intensify their attacks in major cities, factories and industries, decreasing production and exports from China, and increasing China's security spending (Beckley 2012). China's internal instability shifts government's attention from expanding trade. This policy shift combined with the other factors weaken Africa-China. The continent becomes vulnerable, dependent on peace keeping operations and humanitarian aid as forced migration, displacements and refugees abound, making Africa the failed promise.

IV. POLICY RECOMMENDATIONS

POLICY RECOMMENDATIONS: AFRICA-THE GROWTH ANGEL

Liberia needs to exploit this prosperous global and regional economic environment that has arrived at the end of Liberia Rising Vision 2030 (MOF 2014) to its national advantage. Monrovia should enter into a comprehensive economic partnership agreement with Beijing to guarantee the following. First, Liberia is committed to the One China Policy, and the China Union has invested USD2.6b in Iron Ore mining, the biggest FDI in Liberia (Liberia NIC 2014). Therefore, the government needs to lobby and must attract China's interest free and low interest loans as well as grants to invest heavily in the infrastructural sector by building roads, railways, sea and airports. This will foster growth and development, and increase access to basic services like education, health and water in Liberia. Second, Liberia should lure more Chinese investment in the agriculture sector to increase agriculture output and productivity. This might result into food security and increase export of agricultural products from Liberia. Third, the government should use its bilateral proximity to China to open three industrial zones in the three main regions of the country. These zones will serve as growth corridors in which manufacturing of raw materials would occur for export. Increased export will offset any negative balance of trade Liberia and create trade surplus. Fourth, government should sign a bilateral education exchange agreement under which Liberian students will study in China in the technical areas.

POLICY RECOMMENDATIONS: AFRICA- THE FAILING PROMISE

Amidst economic decline and increasing instability in Africa, Liberia's infrastructural projects mainly supported by China might falter. Instability in other neighbouring states may threaten Liberia's national security. The government should therefore readjust its foreign policy objectives. Government should seek greater participation in the United States' African Growth and Opportunity Act free tread agreement signed into law on May

18, 2000 (http://trade.gov/agoa/). As this Act offers tangible incentives for African countries to open their economies and build free markets, it would be in the country's interest to shift focus from Chinese investments and focus on US markets, investment and trade. The government should also advance the EU-Liberia dialogue (MFA 2014) into pragmatic engagement by agreeing and signing a comprehensive trade and partnership agreement with the European Union. The US and EU markets would compensate for the lost Chinese trade and investment.

Moreover, Liberia should be strategic in its interactions with unstable friendly African states. The government should advocate, through the AU Commission, for increased international support to peacekeeping and peacebuilding operations on the continent. China, for its part, should support international peace operations in Africa to safeguard existing Chinese investments on the continent. Although national security is not the focal of this policy memo, instability in most parts of Africa threaten security in Liberia. The government should therefore engage the US State Department to provide strategic support to the Armed Forces of Liberia (AFL) and other paramilitary apparatuses. This will help Liberia to mitigate any insecurity risks that might arise.

V.   EARLY WARNING INDICATORS

EARLY WARNING INDICATORS: AFRICA-THE GROWTH ANGEL

Several early warning indicators for this scenario will come to pass signalling that the scenario is evolving. In 2020, Africa's combined real GDP growth rate rises to 10 per cent and reaches 12 per cent in 2025. Current Africa-China trade of USD210.2b (Xinhua Global Times 2014) also rises to USD280b netting an increase of USD70b by 2020 and USD350b in 2025. By 2020, most parts of Africa are peaceful and stable. All African states have acceded to the APRM by 2020 and have also signed and ratified the African Charter on Human and People's Rights by 2025.

EARLY WARNING INDICATORS: AFRICA- THE FAILING PROMISE

There are a number of early warning indicators for this scenario. By 2020 the Federal Republic of Nigeria, Africa's biggest economy and West Africa's security giant (ECOWAS 2013) is engulfed in the flames of a civil conflict. Africa's economic growth in 2025 declines to 4.0 per cent. In 2020, the projected US oil and gas boom arrives, overshadowing supplies mainly from Africa (Blackwill & O'Sullivan 2014).

REFERENCES

ABC News 2014, Australia

Africa Development Bank (AfDB) 2012

Africa Infrastructure Country Diagnostic Report 2010, *Liberia Infrastructure, A continental Perspective*, viewed 7 May 2014, <http://siteresources.worldbank.org/INTAFRICA/Resources/Liberia-Country_Report_03.2011.pdf>.

African Union Commission 2014, *Africa's Strategic Partnerships 2009*, viewed 25 March 2014, <http://au.int/en/partnerships>.

__________, *African Union Strategic Plan 2009-2012*, viewed 1 April 2014, <http://au.int/en/about/vision>.

African Union Summit 2014, *Assembly decision on the report of the peace and Security Council on its activities and the state of peace and security in Africa*, African Union Commission, viewed 12 April 2014, <http://www.au.int/en/sites/default/files/Assembly%20AU%20Dec%20490-516%20%28XXII%29%20_E.pdf>.

African Union Peace and Security Council 2014, African Union Commission, < http://www.peaceau.org/en/>.

Blackwill, R & O'Sullivan, M 2014, America's edge: the geopolitical consequences of the shale revolution, Foreign Affairs, Council of Foreign Relations, United States of America. <http://www.foreignaffairs.com/print/137878>.

BBC World Service, Focus on Africa Magazine 2014

Chaponniere, J 2009, 'Chinese aid to Africa, origins, forms and issues' in M Dijk (ed.), *The new presence of China in Africa*, Amsterdam University Press, Netherlands.

Davies, M, Edinger, H, Tay N & Naidu, S 2008, 'How China delivers development assistance to Africa', *Centre for Chinese Studies*, University of Stellenbosch, South Africa.

Drummond, P & Xue, L 2013, 'Africa's rising exposure to China: how large are spill overs through trade?', Washington DC.

Economic Community of West African States (ECOWAS) 2013

Enuka, C 2011, 'The forum on China-Africa cooperation (FOCAC): a framework for China's re-engagement with Africa in the 21st Century', *Institute of International Studies Journal e-Bangi*, vol. 6, no. 2, pp. 220-231.

Forum on Chian-Africa cooperation 2012, *The fifth ministerial conference of the forum on China-Africa cooperation Beijing action plan* (2013–2015), viewed 8 April 2014,
<http://www.voltairenet.org/article175401.html>.

Government of Liberia, Ministry of Foreign Affairs 2014, Republic of Liberia, viewed 25 May 2014,
<http://www.mofa.gov.lr/public2/2press.php?news_id=1002&related=7&pg=sp>.

International Monetary Fund 2014, *Global economic prospects*, International Monetary Fund, Sub-Sahara Africa.

Lind, J 2011, 'Democratization and stability in East Asia', *International Studies Quarterly*, vol. 55, pp. 409-36.

Lyakurwa, W 2009, 'Prospects for economic governance: resilient pro-poor growth', African Economic Research Consortium, *Foresight*, vol. 11, no. 4, pp. 66-81.

The People's Republic of China 2014Ministry of Foreign Affairs 2014, China, viewed 25 May 2014, <http://www.fmprc.gov.cn/mfa_eng/zxxx_662805/t1151542.shtml>.

__________, *China-African Policy 2006* viewed 8 April, <http://english. peopledaily.com.cn/200601/12/eng20060112_234894.html>.

__________, *China-Africa Economic and Trade Cooperation 2013*, Information Office of the State Council, PRC.

The World Bank 2014, *Global economic prospects*, The World Bank, viewed 7 April 2014, <http://www.worldbank.org/en/publication/global-economic-prospects>.

__________, *Africa's-pulse-brochure 2013*, The World Bank, vol. 8, no. 1, viewed 6 April 2014, <www.worldbank.org/content/dam/Worldbank/document/Africa/Report/ Africas-Pulse-brochure_Vol8.pdf>.

The United States Government, *African Growth and Opportunity Act 2000*, USA, viewed 24 May 2014, <photos.state.gov/.../P_AfricanGrowthandOpportunityAct_English.pdf>.

Tull, D 2006, 'China's Engagement in Africa: Scope, Significance and Consequences', *The Journal of Modern African Studies*, vol. 44, no. 3, pp. 459-479.

United Nations 2012, *World population prospects: medium fertility variant*, United Nations, viewed 15 April 2014, <http://esa.un.org/wpp/ Documentation/pdf/WPP2012_%2520KEY%2520FINDINGS.pdf>.

United Nations 2014, *World economic situation and prospects*, The United Nations, viewed 8 April 2014, <www.un.org/en/development/desa/policy/ wesp/wesp_current/2014Chap1_en.pdf>.

United States National Intelligence Council 2012, *Global trends 2030: alternative worlds*, USA.

Wen, P 2014, 'Internet behind terrorism in China, including Kunming railway massacre: Xinjiang leader', *The Sydney Morning Herald* (online edition), 7 March, viewed 14 April 2014, <http://www.smh.com.au/world/internet-behind-terrorism-in-china-including-kunming-railway-massacre-xinjiang-leader-20140307-hvghi.html#ixzz2yvtqKBpw>.

Xinhua Global Times 2013, 'China-Africa economic and trade cooperation', Information office of the State Council, People's Republic of China, viewed 8 April 2014, <www.safpi.org/sites/default/files/publications/China-AfricaEconomicandTradeCooperation.pdf>.

Xinhua Global Times 2014 (April 22), viewed 24 May 2014, <http://news.xinhuanet.com/english/africa/2014-04/22/c_133281845.htm>.

Thomas Kaydor, Jr.

Domesticating the Sustainable Development Goals in Liberia:

A Call to Urgently Act

On 25 September 2015, 193 Heads of State and Government agreed upon a set of <u>Sustainable Development Goals (SDGs)</u> to set the world on a path towards a more inclusive, environmentally responsible society, which protects both people and planet.

The SDGs document is one of the outcomes of the Rio+20 Conference held in June 2012. The Report of the Open Working Group on Sustainable Development Goals provided 17 Goals and 169 Targets as the next set of goals to be implemented by countries as a means to address the myriad of challenges around poverty, inequalities, climate change, and economic stagnation; among others. These goals and targets were negotiated during the eight rounds of Intergovernmental Negotiations in New York, and finally endorsed by Heads of State and Government on 25 September 2015.

Renowned global religious leaders, including Pope Francis, high-profile celebrities, civil society and the general public worldwide, have welcomed this momentous commitment to fifteen years of global development up 2030.

Since the adoption and declaration of the SDGs, world leaders and their governments are shifting their attention to implementation; however, important questions arise such as how do individual countries implement the <u>17 ambitious SDGs and achieve the 169</u> targets? How do states prioritize the SDGs when governments are changing, and attention is given political cycles? How can nations achieve the ambitious goals amidst limited resources? And what success will look like come 2030, at their end date?

While Liberia, a country whose President was one of the Heads of State and Government on the High Level Panel that formulated the Post 2015 Development Agenda, remains lost on how to roll out the domestication of the SDGs, Colombia 'has been heralded as a poster-child for the SDGs since <u>President Juan Manuel Santos approved a Decree (No.280)</u> establishing the creation of an <u>Inter-Agency Commission</u> for the Preparation and Effective Implementation of the Post- 2015 Development Agenda and the

SDGs'. According to the Associate Director, Sustainable Development Solutions Network, Jessica Espey, 'the Decree was passed in February 2015, long before the SDGs were formally endorsed, demonstrating Colombia's dedication to the agenda'.

She asserts that 'Agreements made by the Commission thus far include the necessity to work across Ministries and sectors in order to achieve this integrated agenda, as demonstrated by the composition of the Inter-Agency Commission; to launch a multi-stakeholder consultative process to identify priorities and to help design the national monitoring process; to launch a process for localizing the agenda to different regions and municipalities; and to focus much of the attention on designing a comprehensive national implementation monitoring framework'. The Government of Liberia, for its part, has yet to set up any such inter-agency or inter-ministerial team to advance the domestication of the SDGs, a process that requires realignment of the Agenda for Transformation (AfT), and the Vision 2030 with the SDGs and targets. For the benefit of the public the SDGs are:

The SDGs

Presently, the prioritizing of the goals remains a challenge after the official signing and declaration of the SDGs. The most recent paper by CEPEI and ODI highlight that 'the Columbian Commission is wrestling with a series of tedious questions. Most important amongst the lingering questions is 'how such a complex agenda, comprised of <u>17 goals and 169 targets</u>, can be translated into a manageable programmatic strategy'?

In Columbia, "Some within the government seem to favor the priorities articulated in the current national strategy (peace, education and equity) as a gateway to tackling the social, economic and environmental dimensions of the other goals'. In Columbia, for example, 'the national education strategy relates to SDG4, but could also support a reduction in economic and social inequalities (SDGs 5 and 10) and promote the development of strong institutions (SDG 16)' writes Jessica.

Conversely in Liberia, one can neither surmise nor predict what propositions there are on the way forward to realigning national development plans with the SDGs. The AfT has four pillars: Peace, Security and Rule of Law; Infrastructure and Economic Transformation; Human Development;

and Governance and Public Institutions. The United Nations System in Liberia has closely aligned its One UN Programme with these four pillars. Now that the SDGs have been endorsed, there is an urgent need for both the United Nations System and the Government to realign their development plans with the SDGs so that Liberia is not left behind in the implementation process.

While other Columbians prefer 'a more literal plan of action, focused on a specific set of priority SDGs, though with a commitment to realize the others progressively, over time', most Liberians are yet to understand and even know what the SDGs goals and targets are.

Judging from these goals, one can suppose that Liberia needs an Inter-Agency or Inter-Ministerial Committee with an effective and efficient Secretariat to coordinate the implementation of the various goals, collect, collate and integrate data and reports, monitor and report on the scrupulous implementation of the SDGs. Various ministries and agencies would be assigned the task to lead implementation of each goal. For instance, the Ministry of Finance and Development Planning should become the lead ministry but focus on goals 1 and 8; Ministry of Agriculture: goal 2; Ministry of Health: goal 3; Ministry of Education: goal 4; Ministry of Gender: goal 5; and the list goes on. Simply put, ministries and agencies must be assigned goals based on their comparative advantage to lead implementation, monitoring and reporting. This will cut transaction cost and reduce overlaps.

Should this proposal be accepted, the Liberian Institute for Geo-information and Statistics (LISGIS) will need to play a pivotal role in this process. However, what is more worrying is the reported 'exclusion of the Liberian Institute for Geo-information and Statistics (LISGIS) from national development planning processes. A case in point is that the AfT was initially designed, formulated and rolled out before LISGIS was invited to provide a set of indicators for the various targets. This was a mishap. However, amends can be made such that LISGIS becomes fully involved in the domestication processes of the SDGs in Liberia.

Data is development. It is LISGIS that can therefore produce or generate the relevant statistics and national data sets. Hence, such institution must become the fulcrum of disaggregating the SDGs and their targets and reporting on same in Liberia. In Addition to LISGIS, the <u>Liberia Revenue</u>

Authority (LRA) is the lead agency clothed with the responsibility of collecting government's revenue. As the SDGs would largely be funded by domestic resources, it is therefore important to have the LRA fully on board.

Other bodies to be brought on board in the SDGs domestication process should include private companies providing high resolution geospatial data to enable measurement of urban and ecosystem SDG targets; local government representatives, national and local Chambers of Commerce to provide data on economic opportunities, business expansion and associated services (e.g. the expansion of broadband and other ICT networks); private companies and mobile phone operators providing call data records to track various systems or to do crime or development reporting; civil society organizations; and expert groups (including universities, think tanks, pressure groups, the media, community-based organizations, et al.); county, district, chiefdom, clan and municipal authorities supporting local surveys and monitoring to complement national surveys and M&E systems, thereby enabling better disaggregation of the monitoring and reporting in select regions and localities. **The National Legislature must equally digest and own the internationally agreed development goals and allocate quantum domestic resources in the national budget to implement the SDGs' targets in Liberia.**

The United Nations system, bilateral and multilateral partners, donors, and the general population must also be brought on board in the domestication process. As national ownership is important, the SDGs awareness and information campaigns need to begin. Opposition political parties need to begin to read and comprehend the SDGs and know the global commitments made by this government to the people. Being fully aware of the SDGs puts opposition political leaders in a better position to formulate pro-poor development policies in their manifestos. It is not about they and us, the SDGs are for both the government as a duty bearer to implement, and the people as rights holders to demand accountability of the government in delivering these lofty commitments made by governments at the international level.

The necessity to prioritize the SDG agenda 'without cherry-picking only politically palatable issues, to engage local government leaders, and to design a robust and inclusive monitoring system are challenges that many countries around the world', including Liberia, will face over the coming year. There is no one right or wrong answer, but 'Colombia's process helps to shed light on possible scenarios or strategies for overcoming these challenges and to guide the way for other countries'.

Currently, several countries around the world have already started to align their national development plans with the Post-2015 Development Agenda in order to create synergy and convergence for easy implementation. While many countries are preparing to begin their implementation processes at the beginning of 2016, others have begun. For instance, Zimbabwe, Ghana, Mexico, Columbia, and Nepal have started the integration of the Post-2015 Development Plan into their national development agendas.

Despite efforts being made by other countries to nationalize the SDGs, Liberia is frustratingly yet to begin focused discussion on the SDGs domestication and roll out implementation. Government has had excuses for not meeting the MDGs. Many pundits have argued that all countries did not have the same starting conditions, and that Liberia was in Crisis when the MDGs were declared. Unlike the time of the MDGs, Liberia has played a front liner role in the formulation, signing and adoption of the Sustainable Development Goals. President Ellen Johnson Sirleaf served as one of the Heads of State and Government on the UN High Level Panel set up in July 2012 by UN Secretary General Ban Ki Moon to formulate the Post-2015 Development Agenda. She also chaired the African Union High Level Committee on the Post-2015 Development Agenda. The HLC formulated the Common African Position and ensured its integration in the SDGs.

Now that the SDGs have been officially adopted and declared by Heads of State and Government, the Liberian Government has no excuses any longer for not hitting the ground running with the nationalization of the SDGs, and their full implementation. Therefore, this is the time for government to take the appropriate action. The Government must set up an Inter-Agency or Inter-Ministerial Committee to coordinate the implementation and monitoring of and reporting on the SDGs nationally and internationally. A hint to a wise is quite sufficient.

PRESIDENT WEAH MUST PRIORITIZE SDGS IMPLEMENTATION

I. BACKGROUND

In the maiden edition of the Liberian Times Magazine, we urged President Sirleaf's Government to 'set up an Inter-Agency or Inter-Ministerial Committee to coordinate the implementation, monitoring of and reporting on the SDGs nationally and internationally'. Although the Government was not inclined to this, the international community and individual countries are already making tremendous progress. Liberia is behind time in the domestication of the SDGs needless talk about its implementation.

The High-Level Political Forum on Sustainable Development (or "HLPF"), has been meeting at UN Headquarters in New York. The HLPF remains the annual global moment for the UN and development community to review and celebrate progress on the implementation of the SDGs. Although some governments think this forum should be named and styled the "Annual SDG Review Conference", it is nonetheless a key forum for government ministers and other development actors. At this forum, they take stock on current progress, and share lessons learned thus far. This means that the 15-year journey to ending extreme poverty is already in full swing, but without any notable progress in Liberia.

Almost two and half years into 2016, some governments have erected systems to deliver the ambitious and integrated agenda. The HLPF examined and tested new ideas and shared experiences on how their governments are driving the implementation of SDGs. According to the United Nations Foundation, 'harnessing the power of positive recognition of progress and peer learning, the HLPF will help drive national and local implementation and cooperation efforts to achieve the SDGs'.

The major transformations that the SDGs call for will not happen overnight. However, early progress from trailblazing countries has been recorded. Unfortunately, Liberia is nowhere to be found amongst trailblazers. There is positive move towards National Voluntary Reviews. National Voluntary Reviews now provide the space for governments to showcase reviews of their early SDGs progress. In 2016, more 22 countries presented their plans at the HLPF, and in 2017, the number doubled. Their presentations provided a window into how those governments plan to integrate the 2030 Agenda at the national levels. China, Colombia, Egypt, Estonia, Finland, France, Georgia, Germany, Madagascar, Mexico, Montenegro, Morocco, Norway, the Philippines, the Republic of Korea, Samoa, Sierra Leone, Switzerland, Togo, Turkey, Uganda and Venezuela were the first batch of trailblazers.

II.   THE CASE OF LIBERIA

The Republic of Liberia, whose President was one of the three Heads of State and Government on the High-Level Panel that evolved the Post-2015 Global Development Agenda, did not take significant steps towards the implementation of the SDGs in Liberia. President Sirleaf was also Chair of the High-Level Committee of African Heads of State and Government on the Post-2015 Development Agenda. It is therefore embarrassing to have Liberia fallen behind in domesticating the SDGs, needless speak about beginning their full implementation, monitoring and reporting at national and local levels.

The SDGs' first Score Cards released by the United Nations in 2016 and 2017 place Liberia at the bottom of states in the Mano River region relative to progress made in implementing the global development agenda. For instance, in 2016, Liberia had 30 points out of 100 falling far behind Guinea, Sierra Leone, Cote d'Ivoire, Ghana and several other African states. This constitute a dismal failure that must be urgently addressed by the President George Weah CDC led government.

III.   STRATEGIES FOR SDGS IMPLEMENTATION AND SUCCESS STORIES

According to Ms. Madeleine Oliver of the UN Foundation, 'there are many ways for governments to position themselves well to hit the ground running'. Liberia and other developing countries need to therefore adopt some of the strategies highlighted by the UN Foundation. It is therefore expected that President Weah's self-style 'pro-poor' government will immediately put in place the following measures.

First, the Weah's government needs to appoint a lead at the highest political level. For the SDGs to have political and public traction, be prioritized by all parts of the government, increase ownership, and increase the likelihood of a whole of government approach to implementation, it is valuable to drive and track SDGs implementation in the Office of the President.

For instance, Colombia aligned its national development plan with the SDGs and ensured they advance the three pillars of sustainable development. Mexico has a Technical Committee in the President's Office to follow-up and monitor the SDGs. The German Sustainable Development Strategy is implemented by the Federal Cabinet, the State Secretaries' Committee for Sustainable Development, the Sustainable Development Council and the Parliamentary Advisory Council.

For its part, Chad, through its Ministry of Planning, has established a structure or coordination body under the auspices of the Prime Minister's office, with the involvement of sectorial ministries, including the Ministry of Finance and Foreign Affairs. The body consists of technical-level 'focal points' from line agencies (adaptation, trade, etc.), and works closely with the business sector, civil society and representatives of relevant UN system country offices. Chad also appointed 'focal points' in key multilateral and bilateral missions and embassies.

Second, the CDC led government needs to integrate the Sustainable Development Goals into existing national plans. Although it is unclear whether the CDC led government has a national development plan, integrating the SDGs into existing national plans can contextualize them to each country's unique circumstances and provide a national framework for how each ministry plugs in and shares responsibilities.

For instance, Bangladesh has already identified nine of eleven goals in its 7th Five-Year Plan (2016-2020) which are also reflected in the SDGs— the remaining two goals are embedded in the SDGs targets but have been elevated as priorities based on Bangladesh's national context. Colombia aligned its 2014-2018 National Plan of Development with many goals and targets. Sweden has formed a commission to facilitate the integration of the SDGs into a comprehensive national action plan and promote the exchange of information and knowledge between stakeholders. The commission consulted with 30-40 government agencies on how the SDGs fit into their respective fields. Germany aligned its National Sustainability Strategy to the Agenda 2030 goals and targets.

Liberia needs to move beyond the rhetoric of saying that the current government is a pro-poor one. Government must strategically take stock and ensure that agencies and ministries use their comparative advantage to develop Specific, Measurable, Achievable, Realistic, and Timebound (SMART) national targets, outputs and indicators to ensure that each of the goals is disaggregated to align with the national realities on the ground. LISGIS remains the best coordinator of such process in Liberia.

Third, the Weah's government needs to form inter-ministerial mechanisms. Inter-ministerial committees and task forces that bring together representatives from all relevant ministries can help ensure that all parts of government are engaged in and being proactive about implementation. The Ministry of Finance and Development Planning is well situated to play host to the interagency or inter-ministerial Secretariat. Better still, such Secretariat could be set up within the Presidency to give it teeth to bite.

For example, Colombia has formed a high-level commission to lead the SDGs implementation. This Commission is chaired by the national planning department with ministerial support from across the government and other sectors to produce an analysis of existing gaps on SDGs implementation. Also, Germany has established an inter-ministerial State Secretaries' Committee for Sustainable Development chaired by the Head of the Federal Chancellery. The committee is in charge of the German National Sustainability Strategy. This year, the strategy is being updated to make it an essential framework for the implementation of the post-2015 agenda in Germany. The State Secretaries' Committee is composed of all ministries' State Secretaries to ensure that sustainable development is the guiding principle within all policy areas of the German Government. The implementation of the agenda takes place in a cross-cutting, cross-departmental manner.

Additionally, Ghana has established a high level inter-ministerial committee on SDGs to ensure greater coordination among the state agencies for the intergovernmental negotiations as well as the implementation of the

SDGs with sectoral groups working together to build synergies. The United States of America has formed an inter-agency process that includes agencies and departments that address both international and domestic issues to put in place the necessary policies and actions for SDGs implementation. The inter-agency meetings are organized through the White House and engage the National Security Council and Domestic Policy Council.

Fourth, the CDC led government needs to engage the National Legislature in implementation and policymaking. Engaging the Legislature will be integral to leading on good policymaking to create an enabling environment for SDGs implementation, including ensuring that adequate funding is earmarked to achieve the SDGs.

In this premise, Pakistan has transitioned its parliamentary MDG task force to the SDGs and has strengthened the task force's role and functions for SDGs implementation. Germany has formed a Parliamentary Advisory Council on Sustainable Development to provide parliamentary support and evaluate the sustainability impact of federal government activity. In 2016, Liberia set up Committees in the House of Representatives and the Senate to follow up on the SDGs processes. However, these Committees do not have a clear understanding of the SDGs. This is validated by the absence of clear budgetary allocation to implement key SDGs targets in Liberia. There is also no budgetary allocation in the 2016/2017 and 2017/2018 national budgets to fund any SDGs coordination processes in Liberia.

Fifth, government needs to forge partnerships with civil society, the private sector and others to implement and monitor progress: Getting all parts of government and all stakeholders to pull in the same direction and exploit synergies can help ensure that the SDGs are truly transformative.

In this regard, Colombia has built a strong partnership between government, civil society and the international community on the SDGs. Denmark put in place plans for Danish institutions and policymaking to drive innovation and learning internationally. Peru has built a system of participatory monitoring to ensure accountability at the national level and has institutionalized follow-up on the SDGs. Germany has established 'The German Council for Sustainable Development', consisting of outstanding personalities from business, trade unions, other nongovernmental organizations and academia appointed by the Federal Chancellor. The Council advises the government on sustainable development issues and contributes to improving and implementing the German Sustainable Development Strategy and the SDGs. Ghana has launched a platform to promote collaboration and experience sharing among civil society organizations working on the SDGs. The platform has 18 clusters; one for each of the 17 goals and an additional one for advocacy on the SDGs.

Sixth, government needs to make commitments on financing and means of implementation. Taking steps now to follow up on commitments made in the Addis Ababa Action Agenda (Financing for Development conference) and means of implementation targets will help pave the way for early implementation. This requires that the Liberia Revenue Authority must step up its revenue collection mechanisms to raise enough domestic revenues to fund development programmes. It must reduce the various tax waivers granted to concessions and international investments as well as those granted to government entities, officials and several non-governmental organizations.

To achieve this, Bangladesh has increased its rate of domestic resource mobilization by 18% and plans to continue the trend. The Philippines Department of Budget and Management has included a line item in its national budget for SDGs implementation. Liberia has no such line item in the 2017/2018 national budget. Ministries and agencies might therefore find excuses regarding implementation of SDGs targets. Tanzania has scaled up its social safety net program by providing cash transfers to the poorest 4 million Tanzanians (amounting to 2.5% of its national budget). This is just about the total population of the Republic of Liberia amongst which poverty rates are unprecedentedly high.

For its part, the United States committed $50 million to the Global Financing Facility (GFF) to support the scaling up of national strategies and efforts to end preventable child and maternal deaths in the Democratic Republic of the Congo, Ethiopia, Kenya and Tanzania. *As indicated in our previous articles on the SDGs, the National Legislature of Liberia must equally digest and own the internationally agreed development goals and allocate quantum domestic resources in the national budget to implement the SDGs' targets in Liberia.*

Finally, government needs to map existing data and measurement capacity and put systems in place. There is a need for both developed and developing countries to strengthen the quality, availability, accessibility and usability of data to implement and monitor the SDGs. Non-governmental sources of data also present unprecedented opportunities for SDGs implementation and monitoring. However, government must develop strong statistical institutions to ensure ownership of data. Data is development; hence the government needs to empower, equip and adequately fund LISGIS to robustly perform its mandate.

Denmark examined its capacity to measure progress on the SDGs using existing data and determined that approximately one-quarter of the targets could be measured, one-third could be measured with slight adjustments to existing data sets, and one-third would require new measurement systems. Peru built a system of participatory monitoring to ensure accountability. In Liberia, such efforts are unheard of. Therefore, it is time that donors, partners, the civil society and the public hold the CDC led government accountable in this premise.

IV. Conclusion

Although these are just few strategic measures that Liberia and all countries can pursue to fast track strategic implementation, monitoring of, and reporting on the SDGs, countries can develop other innovative ways to implement the SDGs at national and local levels.

Now that other countries have begun full implementation and monitoring of as well as reporting on the SDGs, the Liberian Government has no excuses any longer for not adopting the best practices. Government Must hit the ground running with the nationalization of the SDGs, and their full implementation. The count down to 2015 is already in full swing. Therefore, this is the time to take an affirmative action.

ANNEX I

CRAWFORD SCHOOL'S REFLECTION ON THE AUTHOR

Leading Liberia

29th January 2015

- <u>Crawford School of Public Policy</u>

2014 was a big year for Crawford graduate Thomas Kaydor who celebrated his graduation, published a book and was appointed Deputy Foreign Minister for International Cooperation and Economic Integration of Liberia.

The <u>Master of Public Policy</u> student is no stranger to Liberian politics, previously holding the position of Assistant Minister for Africa, Asia and the Pacific in Liberia before studying at Crawford School.

The President of Liberia appointed Kaydor to his new role on 2 December 2014 - two weeks before his graduation from Asia and the Pacific's leading public policy school. His responsibilities in the Ministry of Foreign Affairs include coordinating all bilateral and multilateral development programs and projects of Liberia.

"Studying at Crawford School prepared me with the strategic skills to manage Liberia's development priorities. I'm confident I'll be able to lead the Liberian Foreign Ministry with the skills I learnt from Crawford School," said Kaydor.

While Kaydor wasn't in Australia for long, he wanted to make the best out of his limited time here – researching, writing and publishing a <u>book on Liberian democracy</u>. He also remained committed to mentoring and encouraging fellow postgraduate students to submit their top essays to be published in the book: *Global Perspectives on International Affairs: a collection of essays.*

"The best thing about studying at Crawford was that I had a chance to combine academic work with research and publication because the School places a lot of emphasis on research - something that helped me achieve my dream of becoming an author," said Kaydor.

Kaydor also volunteered as a Representative for <u>ANU College of Asia and the Pacific</u> in the <u>Postgraduate and Research Students' Association</u> in order to stay connected and represent the ANU student community.

"I cannot measure the value of studying at Crawford in dollars and cents. All I can say is that it is a lifelong and once in a lifetime achievement for anyone to study at such a prestigious school. I think Crawford is the best school in the world," said Kaydor.

He added that the opportunity to study with fellow future global leaders was an honor and provided him with a well-rounded Australian educational experience.

"I came to Crawford as it's a place to refine the capabilities of global and emerging leaders, and as such, it brings together students of diverse backgrounds.

"Crawford is a place for scholars to gain new insights for transforming the world. It presents an arena for leaders to rediscover their capabilities and become original thinkers, creative agents, and the fulcrum for growth and development in society," said Kaydor.

Not wanting to waste any time, a few weeks after graduating and arriving in Liberia, Kaydor sat down to write a detailed strategic plan for his department to ensure he could use his skills from Crawford to help Liberia.

Living in Australia while his family and friends remained in Liberia was challenging, but the biggest hurdle was watching his country suffer, fight and survive the deadly Ebola virus that is devastating Africa.

"I'm grateful for my family to have survived the Ebola virus that ravaged the socio-political and economic fabrics of Liberia, Guinea and Sierra Leone. Today, there are only ten Ebola cases left in Liberia. This is a remarkable achievement. I would like to thank the people and Government of Liberia for battling this virus to a point where the country will soon be declared an Ebola free nation," said Kaydor.

Saying goodbye to Australia was a tough challenge for the proud graduate who remembers his time in Canberra fondly.

"I miss Australia so much. I miss the cordial friendship and warm embrace of the people, the excellent public transport system, the facilities (an elaborate 24-hour economy, fast internet, endless supply of electricity and water) that are easily taken for granted. But seeing these luxuries challenges me as a leader to do my job and advocate and work for a prosperous life for the people of Liberia, Africa and the entire world. If Australia and Australians can thrive, then Liberia and all other countries can also thrive," said Kaydor.

Kaydor's advice to current and future students was simple.

"Students and graduates of Crawford must be the change they wish to see, and they must be leading examples of change and transformation in their communities. Our role is to research, publish and transform lives. Above all, we must keep our connections through the <u>Asia and the Pacific Policy Society</u> with Crawford and ANU. Together we can make the world a safer, secured and prosperous place for all," said Kaydor.

(https://crawford.anu.edu.au/news/5256/leading-liberia)

About the Author

Tom Kaydor, an Assistant Professor at the IBB Graduate School of International Studies, University of Liberia, and Adjunct Professor in the Department of International Development, AME University in Liberia, is the author of "Liberian Democracy: A Critique of Checks and Balances". He holds Master of Public Policy (MPP) specialized in Development Policy from the Crawford School of Public Policy, Australian National University, Master of Arts (MA) in International Relations and Bachelor of Arts (BA) in Political Science from the University of Liberia.

The former United Nations Coordination Analyst in Liberia, and former UN Coordination Adviser in Ethiopia is also author of 'Development and Policy Dialogue: Selected Essays'. He coordinated UN support to democratic governance and state-building. Hon. Kaydor also served as Liberia's Deputy Foreign Minister for International Cooperation and Economic Integration. In that post, he coordinated Liberia's foreign policy, development cooperation, aid coordination, and provided policy advice to the government on Liberia's efforts to curb extreme poverty, achieve economic growth and national development through international cooperation and democratic governance. He also served as Liberia's Assistant Foreign Minister for Africa, Asia and the Pacific, representing Liberia's political and diplomatic affairs in these regions.

Professor Tom Kaydor, an anti-corruption activist, led Liberia's bilateral and multilateral negotiations, regional integration processes, governance, peace and security dialogues et al. at the UN, African Union, the Economic Community for West African States, and the Mano River Union. This made him a policy maker on African and global affairs.

The Political Scientist, Development Specialist and Public Policy Expert was Liberia's Chief Negotiator at the eight rounds of Intergovernmental Negotiations in New York on the Post-2015 Development Agenda, now the Sustainable Development Goals (SDGs). There, he presented several policy papers at the High-Level Committee on the Common African Position, Group of 77 plus China, Least Developed Countries (LDCs), United Nations Economic and Social Council (ECOSOC), et al. He is married to Madam Helen Garbo-Kaydor, CEO of the KONEWA Group of Investments.